The Development Dimension

Innovation for Development Impact

LESSONS FROM THE OECD DEVELOPMENT ASSISTANCE COMMITTEE

OECD
BETTER POLICIES FOR BETTER LIVES

This work is published under the responsibility of the Secretary-General of the OECD. The opinions expressed and arguments employed herein do not necessarily reflect the official views of OECD member countries.

This document, as well as any data and map included herein, are without prejudice to the status of or sovereignty over any territory, to the delimitation of international frontiers and boundaries and to the name of any territory, city or area.

Please cite this publication as:
OECD (2020), *Innovation for Development Impact: Lessons from the OECD Development Assistance Committee*, The Development Dimension, OECD Publishing, Paris, *https://doi.org/10.1787/a9be77b3-en*.

ISBN 978-92-64-84945-7 (print)
ISBN 978-92-64-41178-4 (pdf)

The Development Dimension
ISSN 1990-1380 (print)
ISSN 1990-1372 (online)

Preface

Innovation has been a feature of international co-operation efforts since their very beginning. Even prior to the COVID-19 pandemic, foreign aid saw a growing focus and increasingly urgent calls for innovation, especially in light of the anticipated developmental shortfall in achieving the Sustainable Development Goals (SDGs). The ongoing global pandemic has only further highlighted and deepened the disparity between the available resources and unprecedented levels of developmental and humanitarian needs, and underscored the vital importance of innovation.

Prior to the pandemic, many Development Assistance Committee (DAC) members and partners had started implementing innovation activities across their portfolio, and establishing organisational capacities, systems and processes to facilitate these activities. This work has taken on greater importance in the first few months of 2020, in order to ensure effective responses to the pandemic, as well as to mitigate the wider social, economic and political effects.

The OECD-DAC Peer Learning Exercise on innovation was developed and implemented over the course of 2019 with the aim of strengthening peer learning among DAC members about how innovation work can be strengthened, individually and collectively.

This synthesis report from the peer learning exercise contains much to celebrate. It identifies significant gains from flagship innovation initiatives over the past decade. Numerous innovations have already had transformative effects on the lives of poor and vulnerable people around the world. There has also been a rise in new initiatives and programmes to support innovation, and many promising pilots in every area of development and humanitarian work. Many of these efforts have been supported by DAC members – and it is notable that a number of these have proved essential in international efforts to deal with COVID-19.

At its best, the innovation work DAC donors have led and supported involves the fusion of new technologies and technical advances with new business models and organisational approaches, as well as efforts to reform and transform institutions, norms and political contexts.

When such efforts are at the forefront of development work, there is a win-win-win situation:

- a **win for poor and vulnerable people**, whose needs are better met, their opportunities more meaningfully realised and capabilities more fully capitalised on
- a **win for the development and humanitarian sector as a whole**, bringing creative new approaches to bear on long-standing problems and catalysing organisational transformation
- a **win for donor organisations**, providing the means to demonstrate the transformative effects of their investments, domestically and internationally.

This kind of innovation effort is increasingly not just something nice-to-have for the sector. It is arguably the best pathway for achieving the SDGs and other global commitments. And these lessons have genuine relevance and resonance for the ongoing pandemic response: without attention to the win-win-win set out above, we will not be able to develop and distribute vaccines, treatments or any other COVID-19 innovations to the people who need them most.

It was clear from the peer learning exercise that innovation for development would be of growing importance. In order to realise the broader ambitions of the innovation agenda, and do so in ways that meet the extraordinary circumstances in which the world now finds itself, the DAC membership needs to build on the good work already underway to actively and sustainably encourage, foster, incentivise and manage truly global innovation efforts.

This means supporting innovation not as a hoped-for result or another new sector of work, but as a set of centrally important and cross-cutting strategic capabilities within DAC members and their partners. This means harnessing these capabilities courageously and systematically in pursuit of the most pressing and complex development and humanitarian goals.

This excellent report provides a clear and thorough assessment of the strengths and weaknesses of innovation work to date, sets out the future pathway towards harnessing innovation in development and humanitarian work, and provides robust tools to assessing and improving innovation capabilities individually and collectively.

The events of 2020 show that the need for rigorous, creative and collective innovation to address global problems is clearer and greater than ever.

I hope that the DAC membership and the wider development sector heed this timely call to action, make use of the insights and guidance contained here, and redouble their efforts to realise development and humanitarian goals in creative and novel ways. The poor and vulnerable of the world deserve nothing less from those working to support, enable and empower them.

Jorge Moreira da Silva

Director, Development Co-operation Directorate

Foreword

In 2018 the OECD Development Assistance Committee (DAC) designed and launched its peer learning exercise on innovation for development. Peer learning exercises complement traditional DAC peer reviews, with a focus on learning, knowledge exchange and capacity strengthening. They enable members to come together on issues of shared interest.

This peer learning exercise aims to improve DAC members' capabilities in innovation for development and humanitarian work to achieve the 2030 Agenda whilst maintaining a focus on development effectiveness and leaving no one behind". The report synthesises ideas, lessons and recommendations to inform both those who have already embarked on their innovation journey and those who are about to.

Four countries volunteered to be peer learning focus countries: Australia, France, Sweden and the United Kingdom. These members were analysed and assessed by peer learning facilitator teams led by the lead consultant and accompanied by representatives of other DAC members. All four countries valued the insights provided by this learning exercise as evidenced by the following testimonials.

Australia

In a changing and increasingly connected world, the Department for Foreign Affairs and Trade (DFAT) is committed to transforming the way we work to make Australia stronger, safer and more prosperous, including through our international development activities. The OCED-DAC peer learning exercise on development innovation provided Australia with useful insights into how DFAT can further develop its strategic capability to innovate. We will continue to use innovation across our organisation, including in data analytics, partnerships and working practices to deliver solutions for the most pressing challenges facing the Indo-Pacific region.

Clare Walsh, Deputy Secretary, DFAT

France

France is committed to leverage innovation to reach the Sustainable Development Goals and the objectives of the Paris Agreement. The transformative power of innovation of all forms and shapes, from smallest social innovations to big technological leaps, should be harvested in a methodological and collaborative way. The OECD-DAC peer learning process on innovation built useful bridges with our DAC member counterparts and will allow us to spread best practices, discuss and coordinate our actions and investments. This report and its recommendations will usefully serve our innovation model and our strategic thinking on innovation for development. France has and will continue to take part in this process and promote a model of innovation that leaves no one behind.

Philippe Lacoste, Sustainable Development Director, Ministry for Europe and Foreign Affairs

Sweden

The Swedish International Development Agency (Sida) has embarked on a series of transformations to better achieve our mission and to accelerate the implementation of the 2030 Agenda. Innovation is a critical element in that process. The OECD-DAC peer learning exercise was therefore both very timely and valuable in identifying strengths, challenges and lessons learned, providing input and inspiration for our continued efforts. The rich discussions with DAC members during the mission advanced the peer-to-peer learning and added both energy and insight into Sida's discussions about innovation in the broader development community in Sweden.

Karin Jamtin, Director General, Sida

United Kingdom

The department for International Development (DFID) and the Government of the United Kingdom are putting a strong focus on how we can leverage innovation, including better use of data and technology, as well as new modes of thinking, to deal with complex challenges such as climate change, poverty and gender equality. The OECD-DAC process helped DFID and partners to identify areas for improvements and strengths to build on. The exchanges with OECD colleagues and peers were immensely helpful and provided further motivation and guidance for our transformation agenda. This timely synthesis report provides a clear summary of the both the obstacles and the opportunities faced by the international donor community as a whole, and sets out ideas of how we might work together to realise the transformative potential of innovation.

Richard Clarke, Director General, DFID

Acknowledgements

This report would not have been possible without the sustained and in-depth engagement of the Development Assistance Committee membership, including the four peer learning case study countries (Australia, France, Sweden and the United Kingdom) and the peer learning facilitator countries (Australia, Austria, Canada, France, Iceland, the Netherlands, Switzerland and the United Kingdom). The Strategic Advisory Group provided invaluable guidance and feedback throughout the peer learning exercise, and warm thanks are due to all members: Tom Feeny (International Development Innovation Alliance Secretariat), Jane Haycock (Department of Foreign Affairs and Trade, Australia), Benjamin Kumpf (Department for International Development, United Kingdom), Simon Maxwell (independent), Sophie Maysonnave (Ministry of Europe and Foreign Affairs, France), Alex Roberts (Observatory of Public Sector Innovation, OECD), and Loree Semeluk and France-Carole Duchesneau (Global Affairs Canada).

This report was authored by Ben Ramalingam, under the overall guidance of Rahul Malhotra and Joëlline Bénéfice (OECD Development Co-operation Directorate). The team was assisted by Autumn Lynch. Stacey Bradbury and Stephanie Coic (OECD, DCD) helped to prepare the report for publication.

Table of contents

FIGURES

INFOGRAPHICS

TABLES

Follow OECD Publications on:

http://twitter.com/OECD_Pubs

http://www.facebook.com/OECDPublications

http://www.linkedin.com/groups/OECD-Publications-4645871

http://www.youtube.com/oecdilibrary

http://www.oecd.org/oecddirect/

Abbreviations and acronyms

AFD	Agence Française de Développement (French Development Agency)
CSO	Civil society organisation
DAC	Development Assistance Committee
DFAT	Department of Foreign Affairs and Trade (Australia)
DFID	Department for International Development (United Kingdom)
G7	Group of Seven
GPE	Global Prioritisation Exercise for Humanitarian Research and Innovation
IDIA	International Development Innovation Alliance
iXc	InnovationXchange
OPSI	Observatory of Public Sector Innovation
PLE	Peer learning exercise
SDG	Sustainable Development Goal
Sida	Swedish International Development Agency
USAID	United States Agency for International Development

Executive summary

Over the past two decades, levels of interest and investments in realising the potential of innovation in international development and humanitarian work have grown considerably. Investments in novel approaches and technologies, from vaccines to malnutrition treatments to mobile banking, have transformed the lives of poor and vulnerable people. There are new methods and tools, new teams and departments, new collaborations and partnerships, and new principles and ways of working. There is also a growing realisation that the sector needs to do more than just ask for innovation: it needs to roll up its sleeves and start doing innovation.

This report synthesises the ideas and lessons that have emerged from a peer learning exercise on innovation for development to better understand what needs to be done differently to achieve the 2030 Agenda. It provides recommendations for donors as well as for the wider sector who are interested in ensuring that innovation benefits poor and vulnerable people around the world.

Key findings

The innovation efforts of Development Assistance Committee (DAC) members have a number of **strengths**:

1. Many transformative development and humanitarian efforts have already drawn on innovation approaches and thinking – from cash to microfinance to new vaccines.
2. Among the most advanced members, the innovation approach is becoming more structured, systematic and goal driven, especially at programme and project levels.
3. Pockets of staff and teams feel empowered to take on board novel approaches, practices and ideas, and the language and concepts of innovation are becoming more widespread.
4. Many joint efforts are underway to strengthen innovation for development as a global public good, and the International Development Innovation Alliance (IDIA) network brings together many of the major players across the aid landscape for networking and shared learning.

There are also a number of **opportunities for improvement**:

1. Greater clarity is needed on the goals and ambitions of innovation for development at both institutional and sector-wide levels: what is innovation for, how will it work and why is it important?
2. Gaps – in strategy, governance, management, co-ordination and process – should be addressed to strengthen internal coherence, institutional longevity, collective learning, and the external impact and sustainability of the innovation agenda.
3. Organisational arrangements need strengthening – to improve signals, requirements and agreements between different internal teams and units pushing for similar institutional transformations.
4. More active efforts are needed in evidence and learning, risk management, portfolio learning and management, and scaling, some of which are already underway.

5. The lack of genuine and sustained engagement with the global South is a widespread problem, and should be addressed directly and collectively to ensure that innovation efforts are more relevant, appropriate and build on the best ideas from around the world.

Key recommendations

Individual DAC members should consider the following **recommendations** within their organisations:

- Define a shared vision and strategy for innovation more clearly and explicitly.
- Set out clear incentives and drivers for innovation, with clear entry points for all staff.
- Make innovation the focus of explicit organisational change campaigns.
- Improve governance of innovation at senior management level.
- Develop more coherent and courageous narratives about innovation risk.
- Consider the role of existing partners, as well as actors in and from the global South.
- Invest in innovation skills for new and existing staff members at different levels.
- Ensure stronger and more systematic reflection, evidence, documentation, data and communication.
- Make inclusion of end users and Southern actors a key criterion for assessments.
- Build stronger processes for integrating innovation into mainstream development and humanitarian programming.
- Invest in co-creation processes with new and existing partners in relation to complex intractable challenges.

The DAC membership as a whole could consider the following **recommendations**, in collaboration with existing networks, including the IDIA:

- Work to establish a champions group of senior leaders on innovation for development.
- Provide a standing "hub" or platform to join up, co-ordinate and shape innovation activities across the DAC membership and the wider development sector.
- Develop a shared global narrative/statement on innovation in development and humanitarian work.
- Explore the potential for DAC-wide approaches to tracking and learning from innovation efforts.
- Work to bring actors from the global South into a more central role in the innovation for development ecosystem.
- Work in close collaboration and partnership with key innovation players and networks, externally and internally.
- Facilitate joint efforts across DAC members on radical, anticipatory and transformative innovation.
- Invest in enhanced monitoring, evaluation and learning for innovation efforts.

Infographic 1. Lessons from the OECD Development Assistance Committee

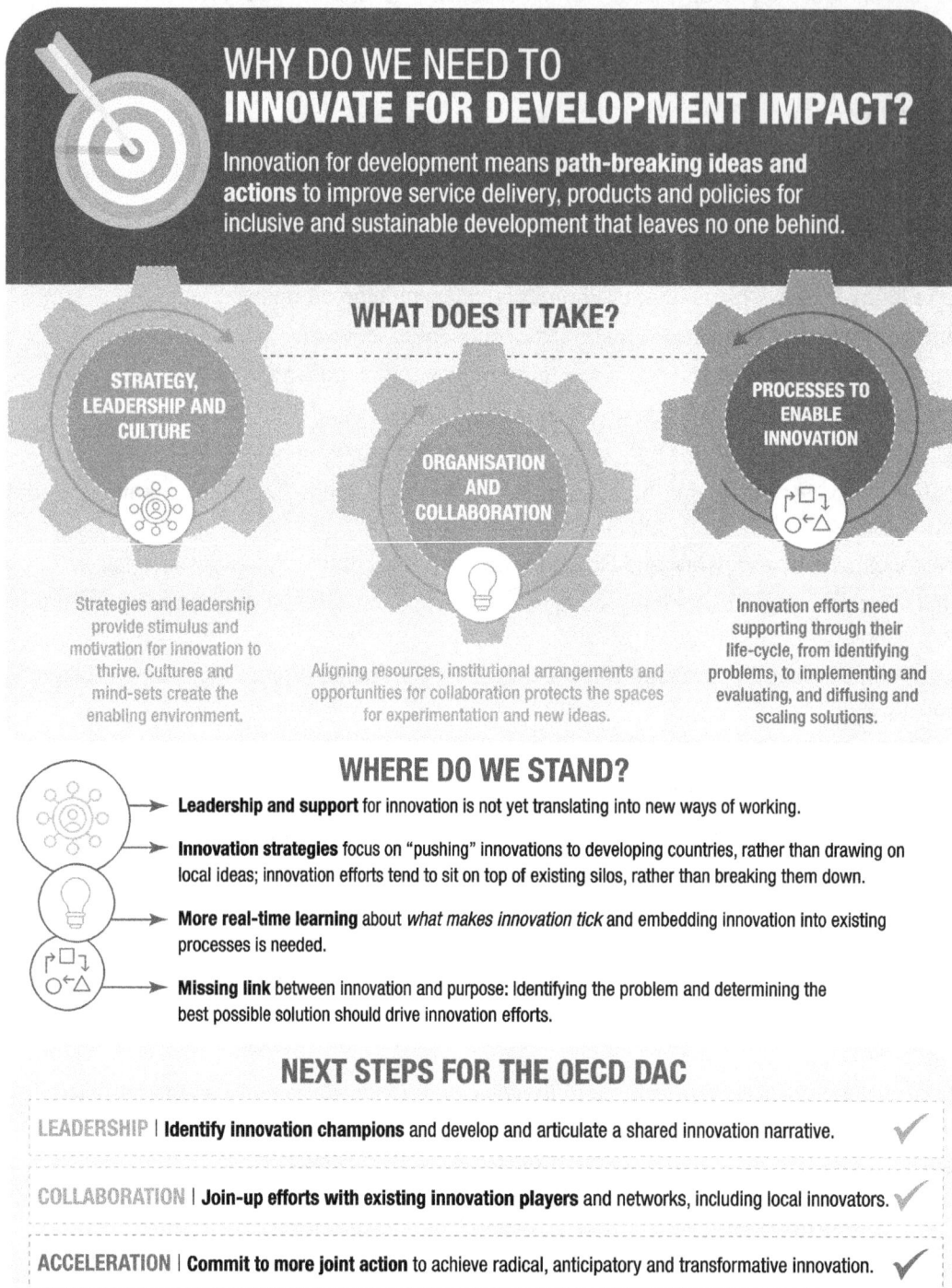

WHY DO WE NEED TO INNOVATE FOR DEVELOPMENT IMPACT?

Innovation for development means **path-breaking ideas and actions** to improve service delivery, products and policies for inclusive and sustainable development that leaves no one behind.

WHAT DOES IT TAKE?

STRATEGY, LEADERSHIP AND CULTURE

ORGANISATION AND COLLABORATION

PROCESSES TO ENABLE INNOVATION

Strategies and leadership provide stimulus and motivation for innovation to thrive. Cultures and mind-sets create the enabling environment.

Aligning resources, institutional arrangements and opportunities for collaboration protects the spaces for experimentation and new ideas.

Innovation efforts need supporting through their life-cycle, from identifying problems, to implementing and evaluating, and diffusing and scaling solutions.

WHERE DO WE STAND?

➤ **Leadership and support** for innovation is not yet translating into new ways of working.

➤ **Innovation strategies** focus on "pushing" innovations to developing countries, rather than drawing on local ideas; innovation efforts tend to sit on top of existing silos, rather than breaking them down.

➤ **More real-time learning** about *what makes innovation tick* and embedding innovation into existing processes is needed.

➤ **Missing link** between innovation and purpose: Identifying the problem and determining the best possible solution should drive innovation efforts.

NEXT STEPS FOR THE OECD DAC

LEADERSHIP | **Identify innovation champions** and develop and articulate a shared innovation narrative. ✓

COLLABORATION | **Join-up efforts with existing innovation players** and networks, including local innovators. ✓

ACCELERATION | **Commit to more joint action** to achieve radical, anticipatory and transformative innovation. ✓

1 Context of the DAC peer learning exercise on innovation for development

Innovation for development and humanitarian work is understood as finance and technologies as well as new policies, partnerships, business models, practices, approaches, behavioural insights and methods of development co-operation across all sectors. This chapter explains the genesis of this peer-learning exercise, a priority challenge which Development Assistance Committee (DAC) members identified as urgently requiring more research and learning during its 2017 High-Level Meeting. It outlines the building blocks for strengthening innovation capabilities: strategy, management and culture; organisation and collaboration for innovation; as well as the innovation process from identification of problems to scaling of approaches.

Context

Innovation has played a role in development and humanitarian efforts throughout the history of international co-operation (Conway and Waage, 2010[1]). In 1867, Henri Dunant, a Swiss businessman, proposed the innovation that would form the basis of modern humanitarian action, arguing for "relief societies for the purpose of having care given by zealous, devoted and thoroughly qualified volunteers" (1939[2]). Some 80 years later, during the speech that launched the modern era of development co-operation, United States President Harry S. Truman, in his 1949 inaugural address, noted that "the material resources which we can afford to use for assistance of other peoples are limited. But our imponderable resources in technical knowledge are constantly growing and are inexhaustible". In the same inaugural address, Truman went on to call for "a bold new program for making the benefits of our scientific advances and industrial progress available for the improvement and growth of underdeveloped nations" (1949[3]).

Over the past two decades, levels of interest and investments in realising the potential of innovation in international development and humanitarian work have grown. In the humanitarian sector, life-saving and life-improving innovations include cash-based programming, community-based approaches to treat malnourished children and new technologies for crisis management (Obrecht and Warner, 2016[4]). The development side of the system has seen half a billion children receive the full course of essential life-saving vaccines, thanks to new biomedical advances that have driven down the cost of medicines, combined with enhanced national systems for vaccine delivery that have themselves benefited from innovative solutions in areas such as logistics and refrigeration.

Elsewhere, the rapid spread of mobile phone-based banking approaches has enabled millions of poor households to access financial services for the first time, helping to smooth their income streams, enhance resilience to shocks and stresses, and move above critical poverty thresholds. Other widespread examples include improved fortified seeds for small-holder farmers, and new renewable energy sources that make for cleaner, more affordable and more sustainable livelihoods for the poorest communities (Ramalingam and Bound, 2016[5]).

This collective effort has captured the imagination of those at the highest levels of international co-operation. In the latter half of the 2010s, major new global agreements for shared development and humanitarian ambitions and efforts were established, all of which placed a strong emphasis on the role of innovation. Within the development sector, the establishment in 2015 of the United Nations Sustainable Development Goals (SDGs) framed innovation efforts as an essential means by which to exploit the unprecedented potential for novel solutions to complex problems humanity collectively faced (Charles and Patel, 2017[6]). The same year saw the establishment of the International Development Innovation Alliance (IDIA) as a collaborative platform across major international agencies, with the shared goal of "actively promoting and advancing innovation as a means to help achieve sustainable development" (IDIA, n.d.[7]). The following year, the Istanbul World Humanitarian Summit made innovation one of the core objectives of the global humanitarian effort, an integral part of how the sector should seek to improve in the future, and meet ever-growing global caseloads (UNGA, 2016[8]). In 2018, innovation for development made it onto the agenda of the G7 under Canada's presidency, with the endorsement of the Whistler Principles to Accelerate Innovation for Development Impact[1].

At their most radical, these calls for enhanced innovation argued for transforming what is done in international co-operation, how and by whom. This is based on the recognition that many of the most important innovations for development come not from the international system, but from those living and working in developing countries around the world.

Alongside these high-profile statements and initiatives calling for innovation as a solution to meet ambitious goals, investments have also been growing in innovation as a process and an activity within international co-operation efforts. For the past decade or so, leading international organisations have made concerted efforts to become better enablers and facilitators of innovation. There is an emerging consensus that international organisations must "adapt if they are to maintain their relevance, reputation and impact" (Ramalingam et al., 2015[9]).

There are new methods and tools, new teams and departments, new collaborations and partnerships, and new principles and ways of working – and a growing realisation that the sector needs to do more than just ask for innovation: it needs to roll up its sleeves and start doing innovation.

In common with every other sector or industry seeking to enhance innovation, challenges remain. These include:

- ensuring development and humanitarian sectors can "repeat the innovation trick"
- identifying, fostering and encouraging the best creative ideas
- working effectively with actors such as the private sector, entrepreneurs, scientists, national governments, civil society, and poor and vulnerable communities
- making consistent and patient investments in the face of complexity and uncertainty
- ensuring effective management of risks
- establishing and maintaining a clear focus on end users and impacts
- scaling new approaches that often challenge vested interests
- making sure innovation is not a short-lived fad, but a transformative catalyst.

Background to this report

The OECD DAC has been working on innovation for development for a number of years (see Figure 1.1 for a timeline of key events in innovation for development and humanitarian assistance). At the 2017 High-Level Meeting, innovation for development and humanitarian work was defined broadly as:

> ... finance and technologies as well as new policies, partnerships, business models, practices, approaches, behavioural insights and methods of development co-operation across all sectors.

Against this background, in 2018 the OECD DAC designed and launched its peer learning exercise (PLE) on innovation for development. Peer learning exercises complement traditional DAC peer reviews, with a focus on learning, knowledge exchange and capacity strengthening. They enable members to come together on issues of shared interest. In the case of the innovation for development exercise, there was a specific desire to enable members to better understand "what needs to be done differently to achieve the 2030 Agenda whilst maintaining a focus on development effectiveness and leaving no one behind."

Figure 1.1. Key sector-wide efforts in innovation for development, 2010-19

2019	• OECD-DAC launches peer learning exercice on innovation for development and organises its first multi-stakeholder event
2018	• Whistler Principles to Accelerate Innovation for Development Impact endorsed by the Group of Seven (G7) countries
2017	• OECD-DAC High-Level Meeting communiqué and DAC Chair Canada hosted roundtable, "Innovations for the 2030 Agenda"
2016	• Nesta UK publishes open-source book on Innovation for Development
2015	• IDIA established; World Bank publishes World Development Report on *Digital Dividends*; DAC Prize for taking development innovation to scale awarded
2014	• Digital Development Principles established; Global Innovation Fund launched
2011-13	• First wave of DAC members set up internal innovation teams and units established
2010	• UNICEF Innovation for Development Principles and Humanitarian Innovation Fund

The overall goal of the PLE was to improve DAC members' capabilities in innovation for development and humanitarian work, with specific attention to improvements in the following areas:

- defining innovation and its value for development co-operation
- identifying enablers and constraints to innovation
- incentivising, managing, delivering and communicating the benefits of innovation
- measuring, tracking and evaluating innovation, evidence of what works and why
- supporting locally driven innovation in partner countries
- scaling innovation in co-ordination with others
- identifying good practices from other sectors, including from across the OECD.

This report synthesises the ideas and lessons that have emerged from this exercise to inform both those who have already embarked on their innovation journey and those who are about to. It provides recommendations for donors and those in the wider sector who are interested in ensuring that innovation benefits poor and vulnerable people around the world.

Methodology

The DAC PLE ran from December 2018 to November 2019 and consisted of the following activities:

- a DAC member survey, which ran from December 2018 to March 2019
- desk research, including grey literature of DAC members and wider innovation literature
- consultations with DAC representatives
- interviews with key stakeholders in the development and humanitarian sectors

- four missions to DAC member capitals in Australia, France, Sweden and the United Kingdom, with in-depth organisational case studies
- a multi-stakeholder workshop in Paris in October 2019 (OECD, 2019[10]).

The design and implementation of the PLE was supported by the Strategic Advisory Group, which consisted of DAC member innovation specialists, representatives of the OECD Observatory of Public Sector Innovation (OPSI) and independent members.

The PLE was launched in December 2018 with the member survey to understand the current state of play across the membership. Out of 30 DAC members, 24 responses were received, which were analysed and used to inform discussions and dialogue with DAC representatives and the Strategic Advisory Group. This helped to further refine and focus the PLE and inform the design of the peer learning instruments.

Broad consultations on the methodology led to the development of a framework for DAC members to reflect on the capabilities of innovation, both as individual members and collectively (Figure 1.2). For the purpose of this report, capabilities can be seen as different abilities needed to foster, generate and manage innovation through the use of internal and external resources. These capabilities, or building blocks for innovation, were then road-tested with DAC members and members of the Strategic Advisory Group.

Figure 1.2. Innovation capabilities framework: The building blocks of innovation for development and humanitarian work

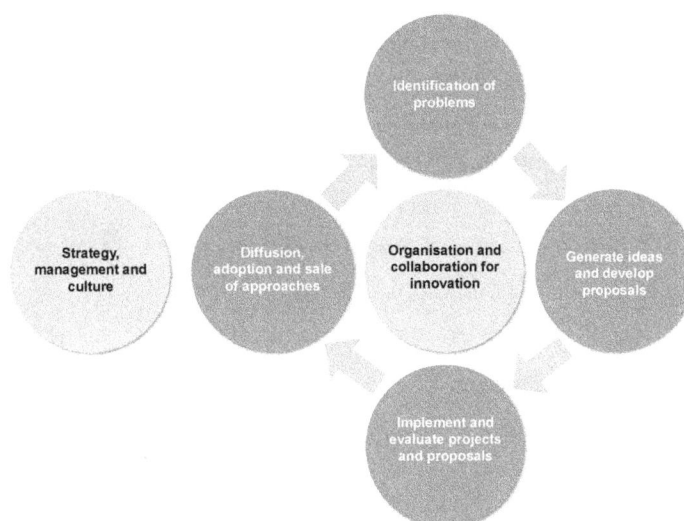

Peer learning focus countries and facilitator countries

Four countries volunteered to be peer learning focus countries: Australia, France, Sweden and the United Kingdom. These members put themselves forward to be the focus of learning missions, to be analysed and assessed by peer learning facilitator teams led by the lead consultant and accompanied by representatives of other DAC members.

In addition to Australia, France, Sweden and the United Kingdom, five countries agreed to play the role of peer learning facilitator countries: Austria, Canada, Iceland, the Netherlands and Switzerland. These members put forward key individuals with a focus on or interest in innovation to be part of the facilitation team, which worked to build a picture of the focus countries' efforts, how they were working and how they might be strengthened.

Missions to the focus countries took place between July 2019 and November 2019, resulting in four in-depth organisational case studies. In addition, a multi-stakeholder workshop was organised in October

2019 at OECD headquarters in Paris. This workshop brought together DAC members, representatives of international and civil society organisations, academia, private sector organisations, innovation specialists, and others. The aim was to foster and inform a productive debate and generate ideas about the current and future role of innovation in the development sector.

Innovation for development has many dimensions that DAC members sought to understand and explore. A number of different capabilities were identified through the member survey and accompanying literature review. The literature review drew on and integrated existing frameworks and models, including OPSI's frameworks on learning for innovation; Nesta UK's work on innovation capabilities and pathways to innovation for development; discussions and substantive work underpinning and resulting in the G7 Whistler Principles; the IDIA's ongoing work on innovation for development; and the Australian Department of Foreign Affairs and Trade (DFAT)'s Innovation Strategy Learning Agenda.

This work helped to identify a number of common capabilities across DAC members (see Figure 1.2). The capabilities for innovation were analysed and grouped into three areas:

- strategy, management and culture (the focus of Chapter 2)
- organisation and collaboration for innovation (Chapter 3)
- the innovation process (Chapter 4), comprising: identification of problems; generation of ideas and development of proposals; implementation and evaluation of innovation projects; and diffusion, adoption and scale of approaches.

The peer learning process made extensive use of the innovation capabilities framework to present ideas, opportunities and options for how innovation might be strengthened in pursuit of development and humanitarian goals, individually and collectively. It was used to:

- structure the overall missions, and orient representatives of both focus and facilitator countries towards a shared language and approach in discussing and thinking about innovation efforts
- guide individual interviews, focus groups and workshops
- structure collective dialogue in the multi-stakeholder workshop in October 2019
- provide a basis for feedback to peer learning focus countries
- inform the framing and structure of the synthesis process, as well as the current report.

The rest of this report is structured as follows:

- Chapters 2-4 provide a synthesis of findings from across the member practices. These chapters place a strong emphasis on evidence from the missions to focus countries and the resulting case studies, while also drawing on the survey findings, wider literature review and interviews.
- Chapter 5 summarises the overall findings, sets out strengths and opportunities from across the focus countries, and presents recommendations for consideration by DAC members at different stages of their innovation journey, as well as across the DAC membership as a whole.

References

Charles, K. and D. Patel (2017), *Estimating the SDGs' Demand for Innovation*, Working Paper [6] 469, Centre for Global Development, Washington, DC, http://www.cgdev.org/sites/default/files/estimating-sdgs-demand-innovation.pdf (accessed on 1 January 2020).

Conway, G. and J. Waage (2010), *Science and Innovation for Development*, UK Collaborative on Development Sciences, https://assets.publishing.service.gov.uk/media/57a08af840f0b652dd0009f2/Science_and_Innovation_introduction.pdf. [1]

Dunant, H. (1939), *A Memory of Solferino*, International Committee of the Red Cross, Geneva, https://www.icrc.org/en/doc/assets/files/publications/icrc-002-0361.pdf. [2]

IDIA (n.d.), *International Development Innovation Alliance website*, http://www.idiainnovation.org/about-idia (accessed on 1 January 2020). [7]

Obrecht, A. and A. Warner (2016), *More Than Just Luck: Innovation in Humanitarian Action*, HIF/ALNAP Study, London, http://www.elrha.org/wp-content/uploads/2015/01/hif-alnap-2016-innovation-more-than-luck.pdf (accessed on 1 January 2020). [4]

OECD (2019), *Accelerating Innovation for Development Impact: Summary Record*, OECD, Paris, http://www.oecd.org/dac/development-assistance-committee/Accelerating-Innovation-for-Development-Impact-Summary-Record.pdf (accessed on 1 January 2020). [10]

Ramalingam, B. and K. Bound (2016), *Innovation for International Development: Navigating the Paths and Pitfalls*, Nesta, https://media.nesta.org.uk/documents/innovation_in_international_development_v7.pdf. [5]

Ramalingam, B. et al. (2015), *Strengthening the Humanitarian Innovation Ecosystem*, University of Brighton, Brighton, https://assets.publishing.service.gov.uk/media/57a08977e5274a31e00000c6/Humanitarian_Innovation_Ecosystem_Research_Project_FINAL_report_with_recommendations.pdf. [9]

Truman, H. (1949), *Inaugural Address, Thursday, January 20, 1949*, http://www.let.rug.nl/usa/presidents/harry-s-truman/inaugural-address-1949.php (accessed on 1 January 2020). [3]

UNGA (2016), *One Humanity: Shared Responsibility*, United Nations General Assembly, New York, https://reliefweb.int/sites/reliefweb.int/files/resources/Secretary-General%27s%20Report%20for%20WHS%202016%20%28Advance%20Unedited%20Draft%29.pdf. [8]

Notes

[1] See www.international.gc.ca/world-monde/international_relations-relations_internationales/g7/documents/2018-05-31-whistler-development-developpement.aspx?lang=eng.

2 Strategy, management and culture to create an enabling environment for innovation

Strategy, leadership and management provide the stimulus for and space in which innovation approaches can flourish and thrive while cultures, capacities and mindsets create an enabling environment for innovation efforts. This chapter looks at how innovation features in OECD Development Assistance Committee (DAC) members' institutional ambitions, strategies and policy statements. While leadership support for innovation has been strong at the level of policies, statements and speeches, the chapter identifies scope for more comprehensive support for new ways of working and behaviours. The chapter also identifies the aspects in the organisational culture of DAC members that support creative and novel approaches and those that need improvement to establish innovative organisations.

Key messages

Innovation is increasingly included in the overarching institutional ambitions of DAC members in relation to their development co-operation and humanitarian assistance efforts. This chapter explores the strategic intentions, managerial approaches and organisational culture that support innovation among DAC members.

- Strategy, leadership and management provide the stimulus for innovation and the motivation and space in which innovation approaches can flourish and thrive. Organisational cultures, capacities and mindsets create an enabling environment for innovation efforts.

- Innovation features explicitly and implicitly as part of many DAC members' institutional ambitions, strategies and policy statements. There is a spectrum of strategic progress across the DAC membership, covering emerging experimenters, fast developers and established integrators. Innovation plays a number of roles, including: using scarce resources more efficiently and effectively, maximising impact on intended beneficiaries, capitalising on new technologies, accessing ideas from outside the development and humanitarian sector, and transforming international co-operation efforts.

- There are many strategic and thematic silos within DAC members, and innovation has sat on top of these silos rather than being used as a means of bridging them. There are also silos between innovation-related efforts, and between innovation efforts and the "mainstream" efforts of DAC member organisations.

- Many innovation strategies are based on an implicit assumption of "innovation push" to developing countries, as opposed to "innovation facilitation" with and for actors in developing countries.

- Leadership support for innovation has been strong at the level of policies, statements and speeches, but has not always translated into comprehensive support for new ways of working, new behaviours and new processes.

- There is no single organisational culture of innovation among DAC members. Instead, multiple alternative cultures can be observed – some supporting innovation, but others opposing it.

- Innovation skills and capacity development mechanisms have been ad hoc and limited by resource constraints. More has been invested in establishing innovation programmes and activities, and less in the capacities needed to be an innovative organisation.

How do strategy, leadership and management work to foster innovation?

Strategy, leadership and management provide the stimulus for innovation and create the enabling environment in which innovation mindsets and approaches can flourish and thrive. This includes helping to create the context for innovation, encouraging and incentivising participation, fostering a culture where novel ideas are generated and followed, and investing in supporting systems and processes.

Current state of play

Responses to the DAC survey, DAC member documentation and wider literature suggest that many DAC members have been working on initiatives to design, develop, implement and scale innovative and creative solutions for development and humanitarian assistance. In some cases, this work spans decades and builds on various other related efforts (see Box 2.1).

Box 2.1. Historical examples of innovation from Sweden and France

In the 1980s, several Swedish agencies, including the Swedish International Development Agency (Sida), funded research that immunologists Jan Holmgren and Ann-Marie Svennerholm conducted at the Sahlgrenska University Hospital in Gothenburg. Working with researchers at the International Centre for Diarrhoeal Disease Research, Bangladesh (icddr,b), they developed the first cholera vaccine, although for many years it was predominately only used by travellers to areas where cholera was present.

Thanks to collaboration with pharmaceutical companies in India, Korea and Viet Nam, the vaccine was further developed and manufactured, with a focus on producing a safe, effective and cheap vaccine that poor communities could access. Swedish development co-operation supported each step of the research and development process, from initial discovery to testing, piloting, commercialisation, pro-poor adaptations, international approval, pre-WHO qualification, production and global distribution. In 2019, Holmgren and John D. Clemens, Director of icddr,b, were awarded the Prince Mahidol Award, one of the world's most prestigious global health awards (Sida, 2019[1]).

Unitaid is an innovative global health initiative largely financed by a levy on air tickets. Established in 2006, it provides sustainable funding to tackle inefficiencies in markets for medicines, diagnostics and prevention of HIV/AIDS, tuberculosis and malaria in the global South. Since 2006, Unitaid has provided funding to implementing partners to carry out 24 projects, and has committed over USD 2 billion. An independent evaluation in 2012 found that Unitaid's achievements "would not have been possible without strong leadership from France". In particular, the French Ministry of Foreign Affairs led the way in advocating for and establishing the cross-country airline tax, which contributes two-thirds of Unitaid's budget, and French direct contributions make up more than half of Unitaid's total budget. As well as being an innovative financing mechanism, Unitaid itself is a supporter and amplifier of innovation. By investing in the most promising innovations in prevention, diagnosis and treatment, Unitaid is speeding up adoption of the most effective and least expensive tools and solutions, increasing the impact of supported programmes. Recent research shows that EUR 1 invested by Unitaid yields a return of seven to ten times the initial investment (Unitaid, 2018[2]).

As these two examples illustrate, innovation efforts have linkages to other efforts to improve on and enhance Development Assistance Committee (DAC) members' work. These include:

- collective action and advocacy across DAC members and more widely (as in the Unitaid case)
- science for development/research for development – investment is furthering knowledge and capacity through systematic and purposeful investigation in the global North and South (as in the cholera vaccine case)
- evidence-based development policy and practice, emphasising the skills and capacities of staff within donor agencies to gather, assess and use evidence.

Source: Sida (2019[1]), *Successful Support for Cholera Vaccines Saves Thousands*, www.sida.se/English/press/current-topics-archive/2019/successful-support-for-cholera-vaccines-saves-thousands; Unitaid (2018[2]), *Unitaid: Innovation In Global Health*, https://unitaid.org/unitaid-ar-1617/pdf/Annual-report2016-17.pdf.

While these efforts are clearly of importance and significance, it is evident from the member survey and case studies that innovation has taken on a more explicit focus and institutional relevance in the past decade. Innovation now features explicitly and implicitly as part of many DAC members' institutional ambitions (20 out of 24 survey respondents responded positively). The term can be found in many, if not most, high-level strategies and policy statements, including ministerial statements and speeches, white papers, departmental strategies, and unit-specific strategies, including those relating to sectors, countries and themes.

These references to innovation suggest that across DAC members, there are a number of different roles and functions for innovation, including to:

- use scarce resources more efficiently and effectively
- maximise impact on the intended beneficiaries
- capitalise on new technologies, notably, but not exclusively, digital innovations
- access ideas from outside development, especially from the private sector, but also from science and academia
- transform international co-operation efforts in specific areas and in the way the sector works as a whole.[1]

As well as including innovation as a secondary objective in wider strategies and policies, some members also have innovation-focused statements that set out specific institutional commitments and ambitions. In around a third of responses, this is in the form of explicit strategies, policies or statements that relate to innovation specifically (see Box 2.2). Some of these strategic statements correspond to related areas such as digital development, frontier technologies or data for development.

Box 2.2. The Australian Department of Foreign Affairs and Trade's innovation strategy

Innovation strategy plays out at a number of different levels in the Australian Department of Foreign Affairs and Trade (DFAT), including:

- at the level of the whole of government (Australia Innovates agenda)
- department wide (as articulated in the 2017 white paper Opportunity, Security, Strength)
- the InnovationXchange (iXc) innovation programme (DFAT Innovation Strategy 2018-21 and related learning agenda; see Box 3.5)
- by technology area (e.g. cybersecurity or technology for development)
- by intervention (e.g. a particular innovation effort consisting of a package of interventions)
- by specific experiment (e.g. a particular pilot testing out new approaches).

The current DFAT Innovation Strategy 2018-21 is an exemplar of good practice among DAC members, especially in terms of its:

- explicit use of theories of change and the development of a coherent set of assumptions about how innovation can contribute to institutional change
- focus on enhancing capacities as the means of achieving sustainable improvements in innovation efforts – the approach taken helped to inform the current peer learning exercise.

Source: Australian Department of Foreign Affairs and Trade (2018[3]), *Innovation Strategy: 2018-21*, https://d3qlm9hpgjc8os.cloudfront.net/wp-content/uploads/2018/07/03095158/DFAT-Innovation-Strategy-FINAL.pdf.

Across all the case study organisations, there are numerous examples of senior-level support for more and better innovation in pursuit of organisational objectives and positive impacts on poor and vulnerable communities. These statements have taken on renewed urgency in light of the global agreements discussed in Chapter 1. Specifically, innovation is increasingly framed as essential if the international community is to deliver on the Sustainable Development Goals (SDGs) and meet global humanitarian needs.

Analysis of the survey responses indicated distinct stages of strategic progress across the DAC membership. One can imagine a spectrum, with emerging experimenters at one end, fast developers in the middle and established integrators at the other end (Table 2.1).

Table 2.1. Stages of strategic development in innovation among DAC members

Stage of strategic development	Nature of innovation portfolio
Emerging experimenters – members whose innovation work is relatively recent and small scale; linked to a specific programme or initiative such as health or job creation; they typically do not make innovation the responsibility of a dedicated staff member, but it might be part of a specific role.	**Single niche** – members in this group typically have a narrow set of innovation interventions in established areas such as digital or private sector development, driven by available capacities and resources.
Fast developers – members that have invested in innovation programmes, and in innovation capacity in the form of select flagship programmes and key individuals working to advise and support learning and networking, but are at a relatively early stage of institutional implementation and roll-out.	**Distributed niches** – members in this group typically already have a regional or thematic focus (e.g. the Horn of Africa, humanitarian) or an emphasis on a particular form of innovation (e.g. digital) or stakeholder (e.g. private sector), and overall efforts are aligned with these priorities.
Established integrators – members that have a dedicated team or capability for innovation, and some form of strategic or policy framework, as well as a portfolio of investments in different areas. Increasing attention is spent on evidence and learning for innovation, as well as investing in the skills and capabilities of the department in question.	**Comprehensive** – members in this group have a very broad approach to innovation and see it as a key imperative across the entire portfolio.

Note: This is presented not with the intention of ranking members, but rather to support self-reflection and learning, and is also used to provide tailored recommendations in Chapter 5.

Key issues for consideration

Innovation is often explicitly framed as a means of integrating efforts across institutional silos. In reality, however, strategic efforts in innovation are more often shaped and limited by these silos. For example, innovations in global health are among the most advanced in development and humanitarian work, thanks to significant investment by bilateral, multilateral and philanthropic donors over the past two decades. The lessons from global health innovations have, however, tended to stay anchored within the sub-sector, despite their considerable relevance for other sectors.

Silos are also apparent within and across innovation-related efforts. For many staff not working on innovation directly, innovation is part of an often confusing and interchangeable set of terms, which includes digital, technology, science, research and data. Moreover, there are also many silos between innovation and other functions of the organisation, including closely related and overlapping areas of strategy, policy, foresight and learning. There are clear opportunities to be realised in better joining up these efforts, especially in organisation-wide initiatives such as those focused on developing new strategies or strengthening leadership in the face of uncertainty and complexity.

The wide range of applications of innovation should be seen as a success and testament to the diversity of ways in which innovation ideas are informing development and humanitarian policies and programmes. That said, innovation risks becoming just another buzzword – sprinkled over strategic statements and speeches as a kind of "fairy dust", to add sparkle and excitement. At a conceptual level, this broad usage risks diluting the strategic intent: if everything is labelled innovation, then nothing actually is.

In the context of the case study countries, multiple directions, ideas and approaches to innovation are indicated. Innovation can be about transformational or incremental change; it can focus on specific types of technology or on changes in behaviours and attitudes; and it can be about early-stage experiments or wider systemic transformation. It can focus on specific challenges within an area of development or humanitarian work (e.g. health) or it can be more generally in support of changing the way the sector as a whole works in response to a given challenge (e.g. in fragile states, or gender and empowerment).

This is the inevitable result of operational and thematic decentralisation in the case study countries, and the same phenomenon can also be observed in other areas of DAC members' work. As elsewhere in development and humanitarian work, this multiplicity of uses can lead to confusion among staff about what exactly innovation is, and how and why it works. While not uncommon or necessarily problematic, it poses a challenge where there is no common clarity across an organisation.

This was often the case with innovation: many diverse perspectives were apparent in all of the case study countries, but the general attitude seemed to be to let a thousand innovation flowers bloom, rather than attempting to synthesise or integrate the different approaches.

What is common across many of the strategic innovation approaches reviewed as part of the DAC peer learning exercise (PLE) on innovation for development is that many are based on an implicit assumption of "innovation push" to developing countries, as opposed to "innovation facilitation" with and for actors in developing countries.

While senior managers are making a good case for innovation as a result, across the board their support for innovation as a process is less clear, especially in relation to issues of taking risks and managing failures: despite the leadership's support for innovation at the level of statements and speeches, this has not always translated into comprehensive support for new ways of working and new behaviours.

This is especially apparent in those cases where senior managers place expectations of tangible and fast results from innovation investments, and underestimate the time required to move from promising ideas to development impacts. In some cases, senior leadership engagement with innovation can be erratic and hard to predict, and shaped by personal perspectives. These leadership behaviours can give rise to the impression of innovation efforts as both "pet projects" and somewhat transient.

How do culture, capacity and mindsets drive innovation?

Organisational cultures, capacities and mindsets create the driving force for innovation efforts. An innovation-enabling organisation is one where employees are empowered to innovate, where there is investment in relevant skills and abilities, individually and collectively, and where the prevailing attitudes towards exploring and experimenting are positive and tolerant.

Current state of play

How do organisational cultures support or inhibit innovation?

Across the focus countries, two of the most common reflections the peer learning teams encountered were:

- "We have always been innovative – it has been part of our raison d'être throughout our history."
- "What is innovation really? No one really knows or can explain it."

This apparent contradiction is in part because of the state of innovation in the sector more generally. While innovation management has existed for over a century in the business world, it is relatively new in development and humanitarian work. There is a strong shared belief among "innovation converts" of its potential to transform development and humanitarian practices and results.

Certainly, there is evidence that successful innovations can be transformative for the sector and poor and vulnerable communities around the world. The case study countries point to a number of historic "big wins" in innovation, from behaviour campaigns to vaccines and financial innovations. Numerous initiatives, projects and technical developments are underway across DAC member countries. Staff involved exhibit high levels of passion, motivation and enthusiasm for innovation work. Even when they are not directly involved in the process, many donor staff take special pride in innovation when it works.

That said, DAC members do not always consistently signal the importance and relevance of innovation to staff and partners. It is not clear if the innovation agenda has been anchored in organisational realities or insulated from political trends and fashions.

This also usefully illustrates that there is no single organisational culture around innovation among DAC members. Instead, multiple alternative cultures can be observed – some supporting innovation, others opposing it. While innovation can be seen as an emerging micro-culture, the prevailing organisational cultures in DAC member countries do not generally support creativity and innovation, although there are partial exceptions (see Box 2.3).

Box 2.3. How the Swedish International Development Agency's flexible culture enables innovation

The Swedish International Development Agency (Sida)'s culture has long been recognised among the Development Assistance Committee's membership as one characterised by consensus and compromise, which comes with the consequence of sometimes losing out on ideas due to long consultation processes. In general, though, individuals and groups have the freedom to create their own platforms for change. This applies both within the organisation, and across the development and humanitarian field more widely.

In innovation terms, this means there is a general openness to people developing their own ideas and approaches and testing them out in different settings. There is an openness to taking risks, as long as this is done in a responsible and ethical fashion.

However, this flexibility and autonomy can also make widespread adoption of novel solutions more challenging, as there is no overriding mechanism to push ideas towards an organisation-wide scale.

This is being addressed explicitly in the current Ministry of Foreign Affairs/Sida innovation agenda, with a greater focus on shared learning, building the evidence base for positive changes that result from innovation efforts, and making the case for innovation as an activity and a result, both inside and outside the organisation.

Source: Eriksson, C., B. Forsberg and W. Holmgren (2004[4]), *Organisation Cultures at Sida*, www.sida.se/contentassets/abd946b4bbfc4725aea2aa04002a1807/organisation-cultures-at-sida_2527.pdf.

An important enabler of effective innovation management processes is the organisation's risk appetite. Across the case study countries, it is clear that risk appetite varies considerably within and across organisational levels and units. Just as there is no single innovation culture, there is no single "risk management environment". Instead, the types and levels of risks that are seen as manageable are a matter of individual and collective interpretation and capacity or toleration. Different teams and units have different risk management cultures and mindsets, in part due to "pockets" established by particular senior leaders who are willing to take a chance on new and creative approaches.

So, what is seen as possible in one country or in one sector, for example, might be a result of the specific leadership at country level, or thematic leadership of that group of sector specialists. There is evidence of this across all of the case study countries, where certain individuals were seen as helping to foster a positive enabling environment for innovation, which has changed for the worse since those individuals have moved on.

Across the case studies, a number of good practices on how to navigate the nexus between innovation and risk are evident:

- send clear signals about the importance of managing as opposed to minimising risk
- adjust risk appetite on an ongoing basis
- incorporate risk management into the entire innovation cycle, both at project and programme levels
- develop new competencies in risk management
- monitor risk management effectiveness.

How do individual and collective capacities and mindsets drive innovation?

Across the survey and case studies, DAC members mentioned a range of different capacities and skills:

- Development and humanitarian expertise and experience: innovators need to have – or be able to access – deep understanding of the challenges and problems poor and vulnerable communities face, and have a good sense of the limits and possibilities of existing approaches to dealing with them.
- Innovation programme design and management: to effectively design and oversee new funding schemes and other support mechanisms for innovation.
- Innovation technical backstopping: to provide advice and support to innovation commissioners, innovation programme designers, and managers and innovators.
- Innovation skills: to identify problems, generate ideas and proposals, implement and evaluate innovative projects, diffuse and scale approaches through communication and advocacy, and collaborate and organise for innovation (per the innovation capability framework used for the PLE).

Across each of these areas, work is underway within and across DAC members to strengthen the skills of staff and partners through a range of means, including formal training, coaching, mentoring and networking (see Box 2.4).

> **Box 2.4. The French Development Agency's intrapreneurship scheme**
>
> In 2016, an expansion of the French Development Agency's (Agence Française de Développement, AFD) mandate by the French Ministry of Europe and Foreign Affairs led to more financial resources and new sectoral and geographical fields of intervention. To help achieve this objective, the AFD established its first dedicated innovation team and lab, tasked with accelerating its ability to innovate and make the organisation more agile.
>
> A flagship initiative for the new team was an internal innovation capacity development programme based on ideas of "intrapreneurship". This sought out employees across the organisation with creative ideas for external or internal application, and provided resources and time for the ideas to be piloted. In parallel, it provided training and coaching for chosen intrapreneurs to learn relevant methods, including entrepreneurship, user-centred design, agile working, collaboration and organisational change methods.
>
> As well as strengthening the likelihood of success of the specific innovation efforts, the capacity development programme established networks of internal and external champions dedicated to advancing projects, created networks between intrapreneurs and immersed them in the innovation ecosystem. The programme received a 100% satisfaction rating from the intrapreneurs and has been renewed and expanded for a new cohort of intrapreneurs.
>
> Source: AFD (2019[5]), *The AFD Workshop Accelerating Innovative Projects*, www.afd.fr/en/actualites/afd-workshop-accelerating-innovative-projects.

Key issues for consideration

Innovation has not yet convinced the majority of staff in any DAC member of its value. In some organisations, certain senior managers and frontline staff may support innovation, but there is a "frozen middle". In others, mid-level staff are the source of dynamism and creativity, whereas senior and frontline staff are more ambivalent. While the source of dynamism within the hierarchy varies across organisations, there are no unambiguously positive enabling environments for innovation, where innovation is a clearly accepted part of the organisational mainstream.

Related to this, incentives are not clear at the highest levels in DAC members. There are calls for creative and novel solutions, but not always support for new processes and ways of working, and existing processes do not enable innovation management to be undertaken in a robust, systematic and sustainable manner. Consequently, many staff members are still likely to see innovation as something that is "for others, not for me".

Different types of risk have been conflated in the debate around innovation in DAC members. If one considers the OECD framework on risk management in relation to donors (Figure 2.1), it is clear that innovation risks can fit into the central segment on programmatic risk, but there are also common concerns about how they can lead to institutional risks. There is insufficient clarity about these different types of risk in innovation efforts. Of particular importance when assessing the quality and success of any new approach is the need to consider risk not just from a DAC member perspective, but also in terms of the risks of innovative approaches to end users and institutions in the countries where programmes are implemented.

Figure 2.1. Types of risk Development Assistance Committee members face

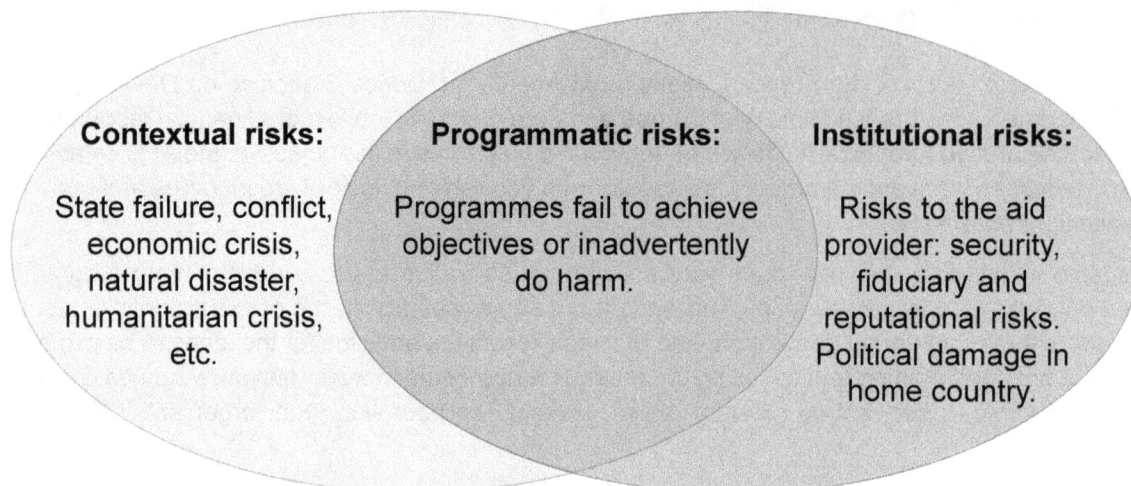

Contextual risks:

State failure, conflict, economic crisis, natural disaster, humanitarian crisis, etc.

Programmatic risks:

Programmes fail to achieve objectives or inadvertently do harm.

Institutional risks:

Risks to the aid provider: security, fiduciary and reputational risks. Political damage in home country.

Source: Williams, G., A. Burke and C. Wille (2014[6]), *Development Assistance and Approaches to Risk in Fragile and Conflict Affected States*, www.oecd.org/dac/conflict-fragility-resilience/docs/2014-10-30%20Approaches%20to%20Risk%20FINAL.pdf.

In some members, experimental risk related to research is tolerated and accepted because it is not linked to specific programmes. In others, integrating research into programmes is seen as a way of mitigating risks. For some organisations, the risks of novel programming approaches are inseparable from institutional risks to reputation and fiduciary issues.

Of particular note are concerns about how concepts and ideas of innovation can be risky in the context of prevailing media attitudes to aid and the domestic political context in many DAC donors. Well-placed concerns about unfair criticisms have made many DAC members more sensitive to external perceptions of innovation. This does not always limit the space for innovation as an output. But it does make donors more concerned to not be seen to be "experimenting with taxpayers' money", increasing risk aversion and making members more likely to support conventional responses as opposed to novel ones. Paradoxically, while appetite for innovation might be increasing, willingness to openly support innovation as a process might be diminishing. This has been addressed directly by some DAC members – with one interesting illustration being how the Department for International Development (DFID) has developed two new categories of risk that relate to the potential downsides of not innovating (see Box 2.5).

Box 2.5. New risk categories currently being tested in DFID's Emerging Policy, Innovation and Capability Team

Risk of stagnation: This refers to the relevance of development policy and programmes in fast-changing contexts. With increasing complexity, uncertainty and ever-increasing pace of change in external contexts, development institutions risk losing efficiency, effectiveness and relevance if practices are not constantly modified, updated and further progressed. To ensure that programmes are effectively delivered and institutions are fit-for-purpose, we need to be aware of external changes that can impact adversely on their outcomes or risk of being perceived as outdated by key stakeholders, including affected populations.

Risk of incrementalism: This risk category refers to efficiency and relevance risks at the portfolio level. It assumes a shared understanding that incremental advancements only will not suffice to achieve the SDGs and mitigate the global climate and biodiversity crisis. As fundamental changes are required on systems levels and breakthrough innovations are required, this risk category aims at critical reflection

---

on the composition of entire portfolios, the explicit and deliberate trade-off of risks, certain rewards, and uncertain radical advancements on systems and single-point solutions levels. To ensure that there is explicit and deliberate balance of risk, ambition levels, targeted time horizons and expected returns at the portfolio level (rather than assessing these elements at the level of an individual investment/programme), we need to assess the portfolio composition and degrees of ambition and risk.

In the private sector, successful innovators are recognised as those who actively and consistently try to remove disablers and barriers to innovation; innovation leadership is as important as innovation management. In DAC members, it is recognised that good managers create the context for innovation. However, there is a desire to embed this in the institutional architecture in some way. This may be a misreading of what makes innovation work and how: it is precisely the human aspects of innovation that need to be strengthened and placed at the heart of the innovation agenda. As noted across all of the case study countries, there is no innovation without people.

There is general acknowledgement that not all programme or technical staff will be innovative, but not much is done about how to address this in different professional areas. Such skills are generally shared through tacit learning approaches, including mentoring and learning by doing.

Innovation commissioning and programme design and management are areas that external consultants and academics often support, as well as in-house innovation specialists. Mechanisms are emerging where those running particular funds come together to share lessons and experiences; the Sida Challenge Fund Learning Group is a good example. In particular, the trade-offs between learning and accountability that all programme managers overseeing a portfolio of investments face become very sharp in the context of innovation efforts, where more risks need to be taken and adequately managed.

Dedicated innovation teams in the case study countries typically balance innovation commissioning and programme management with technical advisory work. In general, these skills are not invested in. In particular, investment in organisational capacity for technical advice and support has not taken into account potential demand from across the organisations, so core innovation teams are considerably overstretched.

In general, much skills development has been in specific innovation areas, enabling staff to better understand how innovation processes work and how they can be implemented. There has also been investment in related areas of skills such as agile, user-centred design, etc. (as shown in Box 2.4). In general, however, these innovation skills and capacity development mechanisms have been ad hoc and limited by resource constraints. In general, the case study organisations have invested more in establishing innovation programmes and activities, and rather less in the capacities needed to be an innovative organisation.

As this work is currently structured and supported, therefore, it risks creating a two-tier system of innovation specialists with deep knowledge and generalists with little knowledge. Capacity for innovation needs to be considered more broadly than in terms of training alone. There are many opportunities and spaces to strengthen formal and informal learning, and to establish institutionalised mechanisms for strengthening staff capacity. These include:

- mentoring innovators and innovation leaders and enablers
- learning by doing on innovation projects and programmes
- staff exchanges across sectors and to/from external organisations
- cross-initiative learning across major innovation investments.

References

AFD (2019), *The AFD Workshop Accelerating Innovative Projects*, French Development Agency, Paris, http://www.afd.fr/en/actualites/afd-workshop-accelerating-innovative-projects (accessed on 1 January 2020). [5]

Australian Department of Foreign Affairs and Trade (2018), *Innovation Strategy 2018-21*, Australia Department of Foreign Affairs and Trade, Barton, ACT, https://d3qlm9hpqjc8os.cloudfront.net/wp-content/uploads/2018/07/03095158/DFAT-Innovation-Strategy-FINAL.pdf (accessed on 1 January 2020). [3]

Eriksson, C., B. Forsberg and W. Holmgren (2004), *Organisation Cultures at Sida*, Swedish International Development Agency, Stockholm, http://www.sida.se/contentassets/abd946b4bbfc4725aea2aa04002a1807/organisation-cultures-at-sida_2527.pdf (accessed on 1 January 2020). [4]

Sida (2019), *Successful Support for Cholera Vaccines Saves Thousands*, Swedish International Development Cooperation Agency, Stockholm, http://www.sida.se/English/press/current-topics-archive/2019/successful-support-for-cholera-vaccines-saves-thousands (accessed on 1 January 2020). [1]

Unitaid (2018), *Unitaid: Innovation In Global Health*, Annual Report 2016-2014, Unitaid, Vernier, Switzerland, https://unitaid.org/unitaid-ar-1617/pdf/Annual-report2016-17.pdf (accessed on 1 January 2020). [2]

Williams, G., A. Burke and C. Wille (2014), *Development Assistance and Approaches to Risk in Fragile and Conflict Affected States*, OECD, Paris, http://www.oecd.org/dac/conflict-fragility-resilience/docs/2014-10-30%20Approaches%20to%20Risk%20FINAL.pdf (accessed on 1 January 2020). [6]

Notes

[1] These roles and functions occur in approximately equal frequency in member innovation strategies and statements.

3 Organising and collaborating to innovate for development

While innovation has emerged as an imperative, external pressures threaten to close down the space for innovation and experimentation. This chapter looks at how innovation efforts are organised in terms of resources, organisational contexts, dynamics as well as collaboration. It identifies how innovation could be better embedded and promoted in programming, financial and operational processes as well as in staff learning and development approaches. It discusses the role of innovation portfolios to enhance learning and oversight, and to underpin innovation governance and strategic decision-making. The chapter also analyses the tendency to ignore national and local actors and its consequences on the type of innovations that are funded – leading to more incremental innovations that maintain the status quo than transformative approaches that disrupt it.

Key messages

- At the same time as innovation has emerged as an imperative for transforming development and humanitarian efforts, countervailing external pressures are threatening to close down the space for innovation and experimentation. More can be done to ensure alignment and mutual reinforcement between innovation efforts and wider ongoing change efforts.

- There is potential to strengthen how innovation is embedded and promoted in Development Assistance Committee (DAC) member institutions through adjustments and reforms to project and programming processes, country and thematic strategies, staff learning and development approaches, and financial and operational processes.

- More work is needed to strengthen shared understanding and management at the level of overall innovation portfolios, to enhance learning from and oversight of DAC members' innovation investments, and underpin innovation governance and strategic decision making.

- Successful innovation for development means bringing together the public sector, non-profit organisations, end users and corporations. Many DAC members see new kinds of business models as vital to establishing balanced innovation partnerships.

- More outreach is needed within DAC members to ensure innovation is not a top-down, headquarters-driven effort; and to engage country offices at a strategic level, and national/local counterparts.

- A critical blind spot in current innovation efforts is the widespread tendency to ignore national and local actors or not consider them until it is too late. Despite widespread ideas about working with end users in context-specific ways and being participatory and open, in practice, DAC members' work has placed much more emphasis on innovation work by mainstream development and humanitarian actors themselves. This has, in turn, led to more incremental innovations that maintain the status quo than transformative approaches that disrupt it.

How is innovation organised?

Organisation of innovation relates to the direct organisation of innovation efforts, in terms of mobilising and allocating resources to innovation activities, and the wider organisational context within which innovation efforts are embedded: the institutional processes and systems and how aligned these are with innovation efforts.

Current state of play

How do organisations create the enabling environment for innovation?

Innovation faces a complex set of institutional enablers, barriers and constraints within OECD-DAC members. These include the ideas set out in Table 3.1.

Table 3.1. Enablers and barriers to innovation

Enablers	Barriers
Shortfall between Sustainable Development Goal targets/humanitarian needs and current performance of the sector.	Broken or imperfect market for development and humanitarian assistance.
Demands for new development and humanitarian business models, including end user focus and local ownership.	Institutional preference for supply of established approaches over demand for novel, creative ones.
Growing involvement of private sector firms, entrepreneurs, scientists, military and other actors.	Negative attitude to experimentation in development and humanitarian work and fear of negative perceptions.
Rise of new technologies and techniques.	Bureaucracy and risk aversion.
Growing uncertainty and complexity in operational and policy contexts and environments.	Ethical and reputational concerns.

Changes to existing procedures and, in some cases, new organisational arrangements, have been critical to navigate these enablers and barriers, and establish innovation processes and activities within and across donors. In particular, the missions showed that all of the case study countries had reformed and adjusted institutional processes to make them:

- less bureaucratic and simpler in terms of the number of procedural requirements that project ideas, proposals and implementation processes must fulfil
- more flexible and adaptive, attuned to the complex and dynamic nature of development and humanitarian challenges, and to unforeseen changes in circumstances and contexts
- more focused on evidence, learning and results, with a greater emphasis on ensuring that projects and programmes build on what is known, and seek to build on that knowledge through active learning
- more open to collaboration with both the usual and unusual suspects with relevant skills and experience, to achieve development and humanitarian ambitions.

Although these reforms have not always been instigated with innovation efforts in mind, there are examples of "stars being aligned" in the four case study countries (see Box 3.1).

Box 3.1. How the UK Department for International Development's Smart Rules provide institutional support for innovation

The Smart Rules established in 2014 provide the operating framework for the UK Department for International Development (DFID)'s programmes. To eradicate poverty in a complex and fragile world, DFID has set out to transform the way it manages programmes. This is based on an appreciation that delivering results and addressing the underlying causes of poverty and conflict require programmes that can adapt to and influence the local context.

To this end, the Smart Rules seek to provide a clear framework for due diligence throughout the programme cycle (design, delivery, learning and closure). A number of specific elements underpin the Smart Rules:

- Moving from rules to a more principles-based approach, creating deeper ownership and engagement across DFID.
- Directing DFID's effort proportionately towards what matters most (i.e. by removing generic mandatory compliance tasks).
- Simplifying and clarifying mandatory rules, designed to protect taxpayers' money.

Demonstrating the space for discretion where DFID will trust the judgement of frontline staff to innovate, take risks and adapt to realities on the ground.

These changes have supported innovation efforts directly, by providing specific pathways through which innovation programmes and projects can be financed, implemented, scaled and evaluated. There is also evidence of indirect support for these reforms, by providing a more conducive enabling environment for innovators and innovation processes.

Certain supporting and operational functions – such as compliance, legal and procurement functions – are widely perceived to inhibit or limit innovation efforts. Generally, where DAC member systems and processes work effectively and in support of innovation, it appears this has as much to do with exceptions that are made based on informal relationships and trust between would-be innovators and operational and support staff as it does with anything systematic in terms of structure or processes.

How is innovation working as a change process?

Survey respondents noted organisational improvements in their innovation capabilities in the recent past. A more detailed illustration of how such enhancement has worked in practice can be gleaned from the case studies. Over the past five to ten years, each of the case study countries has made progress in its innovation efforts. Reading across the four country case studies and survey findings, a number of distinct and common phases can be discerned:

- Phase 1: New innovation-supporting projects and programmes are designed, funded and implemented, in narrow areas and in a more or less ad hoc fashion (as per the emerging experimenters in Table 2.1).
- Phase 2: Some formal innovation capability is established, with a mandate or scope to co-ordinate and learn from work, and to commission its own work (as per the fast developers in Table 2.1).
- Phase 3: New strategies and capacity development frameworks are designed, seeking to embed innovation as a mainstream capability and to work more on strengthening the innovation ecosystem (as per the established integrators in Table 2.1).

- Phase 4: Focus shifts from a centralised to a decentralised approach, supporting the broader take-up of innovation across the organisation as a whole, with common approaches to strategy, processes and learning (as per the ambitions of many of the case study countries).

Although many staff members spelt out these phases in conversation with the peer learning teams within each of the missions, they were seldom, if at all, explicitly spelt out in any formal document or strategy.

How are innovation efforts structured and delivered?

Across the DAC, innovation is supported in a range of ways. The first and most widespread is the use of financing mechanisms, such as programme funding, dedicated innovation budgets and related expenditure lines, such as for research and learning. These are being deployed in a variety of ways to provide grants, loans and other forms of finance to would-be innovators. This might be direct innovation funding, in the form of early-stage capital for developing new ideas, programme funding to enable implementation and trialling, or investment mechanisms to allow for wider scaling.

Financing can also be indirect, providing resources for specific organisations, sectors or types of individuals to develop abilities to generate, test and diffuse novel approaches to development and humanitarian challenges.

Second, as well as providing finances for institutional capacity strengthening, DAC donors have invested in a number of skills and capacity development mechanisms. These include:

- learning that runs alongside innovation financing mechanisms (e.g. dedicated networking, mentoring or training for recipients of funds)
- learning facilities provided through investment in courses for staff and partners (e.g. learning programmes DAC members invest in so that costs are subsidised for participants)
- learning programmes which are internally focused for staff and on specific aspects of innovation (e.g. digital skills, agile or user-centred design training) or integrated into wider training programmes (e.g. leadership and management training where innovation is one module).

The third common means of support is when a DAC donor establishes in-house teams, hubs or other means of providing technical advisory and support functions. Again, these can be internal, providing support to innovation programme managers, or external, supporting external stakeholders, or some combination thereof. In many cases, these teams also combine roles of direct implementation with enabling and/or supporting innovation programmes and projects (see Box 3.2).

Box 3.2. Global Affairs Canada's Development Innovation Unit

Global Affairs Canada has a Development Innovation Unit that acts as a centre of expertise to drive organisational culture change on innovation for poverty reduction, consistent with the Whistler Principles to Accelerate Innovation for Development Impact. The Unit serves as a catalyst, connector and knowledge disseminator at Global Affairs Canada to foster innovation in international assistance policies, programming and partnerships. It has a diffused model that works to inspire, support, empower and incentivise staff at all levels across the international assistance stream to foster new ways of doing development. The use of networks and communities is central to this. The Unit manages a network of "innovation ambassadors" that come together monthly at the Development Innovation Community of Practice to follow emerging trends in international assistance, learn from implementing partners and champion innovative solutions. This network contributes to building connections, shifting the mindset and to deepening the organisation's collective intelligence on innovation.

There are two typical programmatic modalities for innovation in DAC donors. The first is often a programme or project dedicated to innovation. Programmes will typically involve supporting a portfolio of specific innovation interventions, each of which more narrowly focuses on the design, development and dissemination of specific innovative products and processes. The programme itself might be a grant-making entity, offering innovation resources through open competitions or challenges, or it may provide resources in-house to teams and individuals with an appropriate mix of skills and capacities.

While some of these programmes are limited to a single donor, a growing number of pooled funds have been established across donors with an interest in a particular problem area (Elrha's Humanitarian Innovation Fund, the multi-donor Global Innovation Fund, etc.). Large-scale initiatives that comprise a portfolio of innovations are especially relevant for areas of work that demand more than quick-win solutions, and where there is a need to develop platforms where DAC members can join up better internally and externally to tackle bigger and more complex challenges. These initiatives take the form of public goods efforts in response to large-scale challenges (e.g. accessing cheap vaccines, anticipating infectious diseases, tackling modern slavery, mitigating climate change, etc.).

The second structure is where a programme is established with a broad focus on a particular issue (e.g. non-communicable diseases, urban resilience), sector (e.g. education, energy) or geography (e.g. regional or country-level strategies). In these initiatives, innovation is generally seen as a cross-cutting theme within a wider programme. Such programmes not only provide a test bed and seed funding for innovation, but can also be a platform for taking novel as well as proven ideas to scale.

Outside of such interventions, there are also many examples of DAC members supporting innovation initiatives directly (e.g. developing a new cholera vaccine, investing in specific frontier technologies such as drones). These efforts might be internally focused (e.g. management information systems, new procedures and processes), externally focused (e.g. health, protection), or straddle internal and external aspects (e.g. emerging new technologies).

How does governance of innovation work?

Effective organisation for innovation means establishing appropriate combinations of vertical implementation support, horizontal enabling support and strategic oversight of the overall innovation portfolio. Effective portfolio management means establishing a set of processes for assessing opportunities and needs, selecting and prioritising innovation opportunities, and allocating resources to best achieve innovation goals in line with overall visions and strategies.

In practical terms, this means generating an appropriate quantity, quality and timely flow of information about innovation opportunities and investments, and anchoring this to decision-making processes. Done well, portfolio management helps to:

- learn lessons across a diverse set of investments
- understand the performance of the portfolio against different criteria and trade-offs (e.g. incremental vs. transformation, short term vs. long term, risk vs. reward)
- balance, align and focus the portfolio through the allocation and reallocation of financial and human resources
- develop appropriate messages about the progress of the innovation effort
- assess and manage overall risks.

Shared frameworks and approaches can be useful in ensuring the innovation portfolio management effort is intentional and deliberate, that it adds up to more than the sum of its parts, and that different forms of innovation and types of risk are balanced (see Box 3.3).

Box 3.3. USAID's portfolio management approaches

The United States Agency for International Development (USAID)'s Global Health Bureau is an example of a government organisation that manages its innovation initiatives using an ambition matrix portfolio structure (Figure 3.1). With more than 150 technologies financed in 2018 and 25 transitioning to scale, the agency needs to be disciplined in balancing its investments in more cutting-edge alternatives and methods. It invests 70-90% of its innovation funding in solutions in the "Improving the known" category – which could be categorised as core and adjacent innovations – and 10-30% in "Inventing the new" or transformative innovations.

Figure 3.1. USAID's ambition matrix portfolio

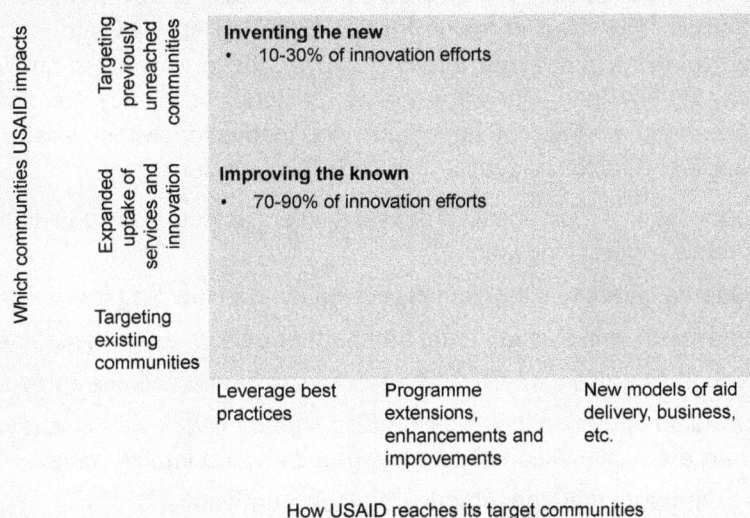

Source: Megersa, K. (2019[1]), *Designing and Managing Innovation Portfolios, Knowledge, Evidence and Learning for Development*, https://assets.publishing.service.gov.uk/media/5da5e56ced915d17bba2c858/662_Designing_and_Managing_Innovation_Portfolios.pdf.

Key issues for consideration

Organisational change in DAC members is seldom rapid, straightforward or unambiguous. It should also be noted that innovation-enabling changes are not the only drivers for change that can be observed across the membership. At the same time as these imperatives for change have emerged from within the sector, countervailing external pressures are threatening to close down the space for innovation and experimentation (as noted in the section "Culture, capacity and mindset" in relation to external perceptions of innovation).

Successful approaches to innovation in the private sector suggest that innovation should be treated as an organisational change process. Within DAC members, more could be done to ensure alignment and mutual reinforcement between innovation efforts and wider ongoing change efforts. Indeed, the organisational aspects of innovation work are often underplayed or not explicitly considered. This is perhaps because innovation efforts have taken more of a "stealth" approach to transforming organisational structure and culture.

There is potential to strengthen how innovation is embedded and promoted in DAC member institutions as a whole. More work could be done to make adjustments and changes to strengthen enablers of innovation and weaken disablers. Staff note there is more space for change that could be exploited, from programming processes to specific country strategies, thematic areas, and staff learning and development approaches.

There are many windows of opportunity for formally and informally signalling the importance of and opportunity for innovation efforts. In particular, because of the role that DAC donors play in commissioning and funding new programmes, there are many opportunities to embed calls and triggers for innovation into core programme and project processes (see Box 3.4).

Box 3.4. Signalling innovation as a priority: Lessons from across the case study countries

Across all the case study countries, there are many examples of creative teams and individuals working to "push" innovation efforts into life through the intelligent and creative design of projects and programmes. In all of the organisations, there were also examples of how the institutions in question were calling for innovation. The most common means for doing so was through senior leadership statements or other articulations of strategic intent. However, these were often ambiguous in terms of who should do innovation, how and with what means. All four case study countries are starting to experiment with establishing windows of opportunity for innovation within existing processes and procedures, to encourage and foster innovation thinking. These include:

- requesting innovation in proposal processes (i.e. asking the question "How will this project/programme support innovation?")
- making innovation a criterion in monitoring, evaluation and learning frameworks
- recognising innovation in individual, team and partner performance assessments
- creating innovation awards internally, and participating in innovation awards externally
- building platforms so operational and back-office staff can work with innovators to rethink how bureaucratic barriers to innovation can be navigated in accountable ways
- learning from peers from other government agencies nationally.

This work can be seen as providing a number of windows of opportunity for mainstreaming innovation thinking into core Development Assistance Committee member processes and can also be used to strengthen related technical skills among programme, research and advisory staff.

Examples of how members have fashioned a strategic function for steering innovation as a whole are limited. In terms of strategic oversight, there is little – if any – assessment of the overall innovation portfolio in DAC members. Some ex post analysis is being done and the International Development Innovation Alliance has provided training for a small subset of DAC donors, but this urgently needs to be strengthened. Without this, innovation risks being a series of disparate efforts going in different directions and not a coherent set of initiatives and intentions.

Fear of bureaucracy should not automatically lead to the dominance of "adhocracy". One area of senior management activity that needs strengthening across the board is at the level of steering, governance and oversight of DAC members' overall portfolio of work. Clearer mechanisms at board or equivalent level are urgently needed to deal with issues of innovation governance and related strategic decision making.

How does collaboration strengthen innovation efforts?

Collaboration in innovation efforts is a vital means of helping innovative organisations gain and share experiences and ideas, as well as undertake more robust and effective innovation processes. This can be in technical areas (e.g. health, water and sanitation, new technologies), key stakeholder knowledge (e.g. partners, competitors end users) and contextual factors (e.g. social norms, political contexts, legal and institutional enablers and barriers). Collaboration adds value by enhancing perspectives, strengthening capacities, co-creating solutions, sharing implementation of innovation processes, and pooling and sharing risks.

Current state of play

Evidence shows that innovation problems and challenges are better defined and understood when actors from different backgrounds – with diverse resources, skill sets and incentives – work together at a number of levels in pursuit of innovation management goals (Snow, 2018[2]).

DAC members pay serious attention to the importance of collaboration and display a refreshing degree of humility about how much they rely on the support and capability of others to be able to innovate.

From the survey of DAC members, a number of different reasons are given for innovation collaborations:

- strategic support to dedicated innovation teams or innovators within donors
- design and delivery of new programmes, mechanisms, modalities
- pooling resources for innovation across the public (donors and more widely) and private sectors
- development and implementation of robust innovation and design processes
- horizon scanning for solutions and products
- fostering and encouraging user and grassroots innovation efforts
- alliances and networks for knowledge sharing and learning.

It can be noted from this list that collaboration can be instrumental and undertaken in pursuit of specific innovation efforts. It can also be more open-ended, to strengthen the development innovation ecosystem as a whole. This last point was especially emphasised at the October 2019 multi-stakeholder conference, where it was noted that "the whole innovation ecosystem in OECD and non-OECD countries must be strengthened", with a particular emphasis on DAC members "support[ing] innovation capabilities within and across countries and build[ing] up collective approaches with a broad range of partners."

As shown in Box 3.5, there are increasingly sophisticated approaches to addressing collaboration issues.

Box 3.5. How the Australian Department of Foreign Affairs and Trade's iXc has established external partnerships for innovation

The Australian Department of Foreign Affairs and Trade (DFAT)'s InnovationXchange (iXc) established a number of external partnerships from 2015 to 2018, including private sector companies, global programmes and philanthropic organisations. The resulting programmes were co-led, and also included co-funding and collaborative thought leadership. Examples include:

- collaborating with Bloomberg Philanthropies on the Data for Health Initiative, which operates in 20 countries, including 7 in the Indo-Pacific
- partnering with Monash University on the World Mosquito Program to develop a new innovative method to eliminate dengue and Zika in Fiji, Kiribati, Sri Lanka and Vanuatu.

iXc was seen by external partners to be solutions-oriented, responsive and a strong thought partner, and iXc staff were typically enthusiastic about their objectives. Partners also noted that the iXc team was characterised by a good management style, ease of grant administration and a clear mandate from the Australian Minister for Foreign Affairs. A number of external partners that were interviewed reported increased strategic alignment with iXc over time, and some noted that they had begun proactively factoring DFAT's priorities into their investment strategies and focus areas.

These external partnerships provided channels for iXc to engage in a range of different contexts and countries, and many were successful in catalysing additional funding in support of programming goals. iXc reports leveraging nearly AUD 60 million in co-funding for the Asia-Pacific region, plus in-kind contributions of expertise and time.

External partnerships were found by an independent review in 2019 to be one of the most successful aspects of the first three years of the DFAT innovation strategy.

Source: Elson, O., T. Feeny and L. Heinkel (2019[3]), *Experimentation, Partnership and Learning: Insights from a Review of the First Three Years of DFAT's InnovationXchange*, www.r4d.org/resources/experimentation-partnership-and-learning-insights-from-a-review-of-the-first-three-years-of-dfats-innovationxchange.

Across both the survey responses and the case studies, the private sector is widely seen as the partner of choice for innovation. This is not straightforward and there are unresolved tensions in DAC members, especially in relation to their respective domestic private sectors and relationships with tied aid. This has led to questions about how best to capitalise on DAC members' domestic national innovation capabilities, which are still being resolved.

Researchers and scientists also play a vital role in innovation for development efforts: in assessing existing approaches; scanning for new ones; designing and testing out pilots; and building the evidence base necessary for scale. Many DAC members have ongoing research partnerships with academic institutions and think tanks, and also have consultancies with them on specific innovation issues. While these partnerships are well-developed and mature, there is often a need to strengthen the feedback loop between the production of research and its use to inform innovation efforts of DAC donors and their partners. Among the case study countries, all invest significantly in research and development, and are seeking to create better linkages between research and programming efforts to ensure the fruits of these investments are capitalised on.

Other donors are key players, as are multilateral agencies with specific shared interests and mandates (e.g. the World Health Organization for health, the United Nations Children's Fund for children, the World Food Programme for nutrition and food security, the World Bank for economic development and financial access, etc.). These partnerships can be specific to particular innovation areas (e.g. funding a new approach to dealing with maternal health) or can be more generically about building multilateral capabilities in innovation.

Across the case study countries, civil society does not play a consistent role in how innovation for development works at present. Sometimes civil society organisations (CSOs) are asked to innovate, but across the case study countries, very few CSOs were pointed to as critical players in innovation efforts. Among the CSO representatives consulted across the case studies, many pointed to a lack of coherent signals from donors, and even to a pronounced tendency for donors to shut down creative and original approaches in favour of predictable and pre-defined goals and approaches. One interesting example of how this has been navigated from across the DAC membership is how Global Affairs Canada has used communities of practice to reach out to and engage with CSOs on innovation issues, and embedded innovation into CSO policy (see Box 3.6).

Box 3.6. Global Affairs Canada's Multi-stakeholder Community of Practice with Civil Society

Global Affairs Canada hosts a collaborative and vibrant dialogue with Canadian civil society organisation (CSO) partners through its Multi-stakeholder Community of Practice (MCOP). The MCOP advances the Canadian development innovation agenda and Global Affairs Canada's profile by supporting collective capacity development through learning and knowledge exchange on good practice, lessons and tools for innovation in international assistance.

Canada's Policy for Civil Society Partnerships for International Assistance sets out an approach for enhancing effective co-operation with Canadian, international and local CSOs to maximise the impact and results of Canada's international assistance and foster a strong civil society sector, which includes an objective on innovation. This innovative engagement and approach with civil society partners has led to a unique process of co-design of the implementation plan and subsequent mutual implementation of the policy. This novel approach has been received very positively by CSO partners, with the sector fully embracing the opportunity to discuss CSO policy implementation in an open and collaborative environment. In 2018, the Canadian Council for International Co-operation undertook research on innovation by learning from national CSO platforms in other DAC members, and used this to set out lessons for Canadian CSOs, concluding that "the biggest risk for CSOs may be to ignore innovation".

Source: Gareau, L. and C. Heshmati-Calderón (2018[4]), *Daring to Take Risk and Fail: Building an Innovation Agenda in Canada's Global Development and Humanitarian Context*, https://ccic.ca/wp-content/uploads/2018/12/Daring-to-Take-Risk-and-Fail-December-2018.pdf.

Key issues for consideration

Many DAC members see new kinds of business models and partnerships as vital to establishing balanced tripartite relationships, which are often as useful as giving the private sector the leading role. Successful innovation for development is as much about the wider public sector, non-profit organisations and end users as it is about corporations. Ideas about the "entrepreneurial state"[1] are starting to filter into the development discourse and should play a role for both DAC members and their counterparts in the global South.

While being careful around issues of tied aid, there are a number of examples of how domestic ecosystems can be harnessed for development gains; for example, by looking for comparative advantages, creating fellowships and knowledge exchanges, and establishing acceleration mechanisms or hubs to address priority areas.

Internally, outreach is needed to ensure innovation is not a top-down, headquarters-driven effort, and engage country offices at the strategic level and national or local counterparts.

A critical blind spot in current innovation efforts is ignoring national and local actors or not thinking about them until it is too late. Despite widespread ideas about working with end users in context-specific ways and being participatory and open, in practice DAC members' work has placed much more emphasis on innovation work by mainstream development and humanitarian actors themselves. This has, in turn, led to a greater emphasis on incremental innovations that maintain the status quo rather than transformative approaches that disrupt it. Earlier and more sustained engagement is needed with innovation actors in developing countries as a matter of course within innovation initiatives and processes.

References

Elson, O., T. Feeny and L. Heinkel (2019), *Experimentation, Partnership and Learning: Insights from a Review of the First Three Years of DFAT's InnovationXchange*, Results for Development, http://www.r4d.org/resources/experimentation-partnership-and-learning-insights-from-a-review-of-the-first-three-years-of-dfats-innovationxchange (accessed on 1 January 2020).   [3]

Gareau, L. and C. Heshmati-Calderón (2018), *Daring to Take Risk and Fail: Building an Innovation Agenda in Canada's Global Development and Humanitarian Context*, Canadian Council for International Co-operation, Vanier, Ontario, https://ccic.ca/wp-content/uploads/2018/12/Daring-to-Take-Risk-and-Fail-December-2018.pdf (accessed on 1 January 2020).   [4]

Megersa, K. (2019), *Designing and Managing Innovation Portfolios*, Knowledge, Evidence and Learning for Development (K4D), https://assets.publishing.service.gov.uk/media/5da5e56ced915d17bba2c858/662_Designing_and_Managing_Innovation_Portfolios.pdf (accessed on 1 January 2020).   [1]

Snow, T. (2018), *Why and How Does Collaboration Drive Innovation in the Public Sector?*, Nesta, http://www.nesta.org.uk/blog/why-and-how-does-collaboration-drive-innovation-public-sector (accessed on 1 January 2020).   [2]

Notes

[1] Based on the landmark work of economist Mariana Mazzucato, this approach argues that, far from being a bureaucracy that should "get out of the way" of private sector creativity, governments can play an active role in fixing market failures and shaping and creating new markets, by actively investing in new technologies and sectors which then provide opportunities for private enterprises and investors.

4 The development innovation process

Successful innovative organisations are those that can identify and direct resources towards specific challenges and opportunities; support and facilitate efforts to search for, invent and develop new ideas; invest resources in implementing and evaluating innovative approaches; and have dedicated resources and processes for diffusing, adopting and scaling. This chapter looks at how this innovation process is implemented across the OECD Development Assistance Committee (DAC) membership and whether an innovation "due diligence" is in place. It analyses the missing dots between early-stage pilots and late-stage scaling and further reflects on the need to think and learn more actively about innovation pathways as they are unfolding. The chapter discusses how DAC members fund parts of an innovation ecosystem and ways to optimise their different investments in a unified innovation approach to pool funds and reduce risks.

Key messages

- Successful innovative organisations are those that can identify and direct resources towards specific challenges, problems and opportunities; support and facilitate efforts to search for, invent and develop new ideas; invest resources in implementing and evaluating innovative approaches; and have dedicated resources and processes for diffusing, adopting and scaling processes.

- Good identification of problems means clearly analysing them, evaluating the pros and cons of existing solutions, and creating space and incentives for novel ones. This kind of innovation "due diligence" among most DAC members is lacking.

- Institutional and political pressures often lead to evidence from problem analyses being set aside in the interests of speedy and timely action. This can often lead to programmes being launched in the heat of the moment, without sufficient attention being paid to their design, assumptions and theories of change.

- Across DAC members as a whole, greater effort is needed to reflect on the end to-end process of innovation efforts and related outcomes. This means connecting the dots between early-stage pilots and late-stage scaling; and thinking and learning more actively about innovation pathways as they are unfolding, and the factors and actors that enable or inhibit them.

- With few exceptions, the development sector has been slow to engage national and local innovators in innovation processes, despite the availability of highly relevant approaches, such as frugal innovation, which tap into the ideas and skills of innovators from the global South.

- While DAC members are tacitly aware of multiple pathways to scale, the rhetoric has been about private sector replication. The reality is that there are many theories of scale, of which this is just one. It is vital that scaling efforts do not focus on just one as the dominant approach. This would be counterproductive for individual innovation efforts, and would undervalue the considerable innovation capabilities within the public and non-profit sectors.

- While DAC members often celebrate effective innovations, these successes do not always lead to more systematic learning about innovation pathways. Building evidence about pathways to scale would benefit from a balanced examination of the successes that have already been achieved.

- DAC members often fund all of the elements of an innovation ecosystem – research, education, skills, scholarships, programmes, partnerships, networks – but do not actively seek to optimise their different investments in a unified innovation approach. Such investment in ecosystems for transformative and anticipatory innovation is something that could be usefully undertaken across donors, to pool funds and reduce risks.

How are problems and opportunities identified?

Research on innovation in a wide range of sectors reveals that while each innovation process is distinctive, common patterns can be discerned in terms of how innovations progress from an initial idea to having an impact on operational and policy responses. According to the member survey, DAC members across the board are aware of innovation "stage gate" processes and their role in moving from idea development to testing at scale. This chapter sets out the lessons learnt from across the DAC membership about how such processes have been established and implemented.

Successful innovative organisations are those that can identify the specific issues, problems and opportunities towards which innovation resources should be directed. In some settings, this builds on awareness of needs, based on those enduring, repeated or emerging areas where standard approaches are coming up short. In other contexts, it is awareness or discovery of a new possible solution that can trigger recognition of the opportunity for innovation. Identification of problems and opportunities requires resources, well-defined processes for analysing problems, and the means of agreeing upon priorities and using these to trigger subsequent efforts in search and discovery.

Current state of play

Across DAC members, the survey and case studies reveal a host of challenges that are seen as priorities for innovation, including health, climate, biodiversity, human rights, disability democracy, governance, gender and humanitarian issues. Some members also see specific technological solutions as important avenues for exploration (e.g. data, digital, frontier technologies, etc.).

Despite the existence of frameworks such as the United Nations' Sustainable Development Goals and departmental development priorities, it is not always clear how different macro-problems are determined to be the focus of organisation-wide innovation efforts. In the absence of more formal mechanisms, a number of factors can be seen as having an influence:

- key individuals: especially at the senior leadership and political level, certain people have considerable influence over what gets innovation attention in terms of investments
- existing organisational capabilities, including in innovation: where particular donors have a strong track record in a given area, they are generally more likely to be open to exploring new possibilities
- engagement of other donors and relevant partners: in some cases, problems are prioritised because of the attention a particular area of work receives, rather than because of the actual development or humanitarian needs involved
- changes in context and need: specific developments such as the climate emergency, new emerging diseases, etc. can drive interest and investment in innovation in particular areas.

Within selected sectors or thematic areas, innovation initiatives among case study countries typically start with a process of consultation to determine what might be relevant areas for innovation to focus on. Such exercises have been wide-ranging, addressing:

- different sectoral issues (e.g. global mental health, better rural sanitation)
- major global challenges (sustainable urbanisation, preventing violence)
- context-specific problems faced in a particular region or country (e.g. how to strengthen human development indicators in United Republic of Tanzania or digital development in the Asia-Pacific region)
- opportunities generated by new technological advances (e.g. frontier technologies).

These prioritisation exercises vary in scope and form, but typically involve some or all of the following:

- in-depth processes of desk research, including literature reviews and syntheses of science and knowledge on a given topic (e.g. the UK Department for International Development [DFID]'s work on water and sanitation innovations)

- consultations with the "usual suspects" inside a given sector and select outsiders (e.g. Grand Challenges efforts in new areas such as conflict and accountability and voice)

- open, crowdsourced approaches that use social media and other technologies to develop priorities from a wide range of stakeholders, including the public (e.g. use of crowdsourcing and similar platforms to identify innovation needs)

- forming expert advisory groups that provide ideas and inputs into setting priorities (e.g. Global Innovation Fund strategic and technical advisory groups).

Key issues for consideration

Across these efforts, three issues consistently emerge. First, the nature of the problems that need innovation vary considerably in their scope. Work on Grand Challenges has identified four distinct kinds of issues:

- business-as-usual problems (e.g. developing a new treatment for childhood diarrhoea)

- big emerging problems (e.g. how to address challenges such as sustainable urban infrastructure or affordable energy use in rural areas)

- systemic transformation problems (e.g. how to move towards green and circular economy efforts across an entire country or sector)

- innovation ecosystem problems (e.g. how to ensure the innovation system itself is working in an effective and inclusive fashion).

While in principle DAC members are willing to work on all of these areas, innovation efforts tend to get more institutional traction in the first area. An understandable emphasis on such "known knowns" can shape prioritisation exercises, influencing the questions that are asked, who they are asked of and the answers that are heard the most loudly.

Second, prioritisation consultations routinely neglect actors in the global South. While in some cases governments and civil society organisations might be represented, the communities living in settings where development and humanitarian innovation will be implemented are seldom, if ever, involved in such efforts. This highlights a critical issue: that DAC donors often seek to develop priorities through consultation, but the reality of poor and vulnerable communities is that more emphasis is needed on active, direct observations and listening (see Box 4.1). Despite continual refrains about user-focused innovation, efforts that build on immersions in community lives are not yet a routine part of how innovation needs are established.

Third, even the most effective prioritisation exercises are not always used fully when it comes to programme design in DAC members. In some cases, this may be because of the necessarily high-level aggregated nature of such efforts: the resulting priorities are often too high level and generic to be put to concrete use. For example, many prioritisation exercises might call for "innovations to enable better community engagement", but this is hardly enough to take decisions about what should be done.

Good identification of problems goes beyond saying "We need innovation for x" to clearly analysing those problems, evaluating the pros and cons of existing solutions, and providing a space for novel solutions. This kind of innovation "due diligence" is mostly noticeable by its absence. Institutional and political pressures often lead to evidence from consultations being set aside in the interests of speedy and timely action. While this might be a pragmatic way of capitalising on windows of opportunity for innovation, it can often lead to programmes being launched in the heat of the moment, without sufficient attention being paid to their design, assumptions and theories of change.

Box 4.1. Elrha's global humanitarian innovation prioritisation process

Major gaps exist in the evidence base and the innovative capacities underpinning humanitarian action. Achieving a humanitarian system that is truly anticipatory and fit for purpose in responding to crises requires building more effective alliances within and between communities of science, research and innovation.

Funded initially by the UK Department for International Development and subsequently by other DAC donors including the United States Agency for International Development (USAID), the leading player in global humanitarian innovation, in 2017 the Elrha network launched the Global Prioritisation Exercise for Humanitarian Research and Innovation (GPE). This is an effort to transform the impact of research and innovation in the humanitarian system. The GPE's aim is to provide public visibility on the range of global investments, capacity and activity in humanitarian research and innovation, and to widely consult and identify shared priorities for further investment and action.

The exercise was initiated with a global mapping, intended to provide a detailed baseline of global humanitarian research and innovation activity, as viewed through published outputs during 2016-17. The data presented revealed not only the range of the thematic, technical and geographic focus of activity during this period, but also mapped the numerous funders and actors active in this space.

These early results raised important questions about how well current investments and activity align with recognised humanitarian priorities and needs, and revealed interesting differences between the focus of research and innovation communities. The data also showed a marked disparity between the geographical locations of funding recipients compared to the geographical focus of the research and innovation activities themselves. The vast majority of research and innovation resources were both provided and received by actors in the global North. This important finding suggests that more needs to be done to shift funding allocations to partners closer to where humanitarian needs are most directly experienced.

Guided by the preliminary results, the second phase of the GPE will be a global consultation with key stakeholders in humanitarian research, evidence and innovation, to identify shared priorities for research and innovation action and investments.

Source: Global Emergency Group et al. (2017[1]), *Global Prioritisation Exercise for Research and Innovation in the Humanitarian System: Phase One Mapping*, www.elrha.org/researchdatabase/global-prioritisation-exercise-research-innovation-humanitarian-system-phase-one-mapping.

How are ideas and proposals generated and developed?

The generation of ideas and development of proposals is a vital part of the innovation process. It typically involves support to and facilitation of activities focusing on searching for, inventing and developing new ideas. It includes scanning of potential solutions to identified problems, prototyping new approaches, and undertaking "proof of concept" assessments. Developing proposals is crucial for turning initial ideas into valid and testable approaches in development and humanitarian contexts.

Current state of play

When it comes to identifying and developing innovative solutions, there is a clear and notable desire to hear from and listen to more stakeholders beyond each given organisation – especially among the private sector, entrepreneurs and scientists. All the survey respondents and case study countries emphasised the importance of establishing relationships with this range of actors in a variety of thematic innovation areas, from health to infrastructure.

A key lesson from across all the case studies is that there are few, if any, innovative solutions that are simply "out there" waiting to be taken up into development and humanitarian contexts. While innovation fairs and similar exercises play an important role in expanding the space for possibilities, almost all of these stakeholders need to undertake a process of iterative learning – with DAC members, implementing partners and counterparts in developing countries, to genuinely understand how their ideas might add value – and a robust and contextually relevant innovation process. This process takes time, resources and patience and is an important reason why innovation efforts in the sector should not be reduced to a "magic bullet" solution: not only is this flawed thinking, but it can also create unrealistic expectations among stakeholders who are new to the sector.

Key issues for consideration

There is again something of a global South blind spot here, in terms of failing to recognise and capitalise on the potential of Southern innovators. This is despite the availability of highly relevant approaches such as frugal innovation, which tap into the ideas and skills of innovators from the global South. With few exceptions, the development sector has been slow to engage national and local innovators in idea generation processes.

Unchecked, the innovation for development effort as it is currently designed and implemented risks placing more emphasis on technology transfer to the global South as opposed to innovation collaboration with those countries. This should be viewed as a significant missed opportunity.

How to implement and evaluate innovation projects and programmes?

This stage of the innovation process relates to how proposed solutions are trialled and piloted and systematically analysed, with the results used to move ideas forward into efforts to scale, or into further adjustment, iteration and testing. Innovative organisations are those which have resources and skills in both the implementation and evaluation of innovative approaches, and a means by which to take successful innovations forward.

Current state of play

Across all the case studies, DAC donors are working on innovation on several levels:

- Micro-level innovation projects directly involve innovators and individuals in specific contexts, providing direct support and investment in areas such as capital, technology, skills, and infrastructure and innovation management processes (e.g. the range of ongoing efforts in blockchain for development or in mobile technology for disease mapping).
- Mid-level programmes piloting a range of similar approaches across various contexts, with the means in place to test and assess progress and impact (e.g. testing out new approaches to community-based sanitation in specific socio-cultural contexts).
- Large-scale programmes that have built on key lessons to scale, and are considering technical and institutional or systems dimensions of diffusion, including finance, legal, regulatory and other conditions (e.g. cash-based programming, digital financial services).

A common finding was that innovation donors struggle to move beyond micro-level initiatives that bundle together such projects. The widely recognised and bemoaned phenomenon of "pilotitis" is testament to this: "[the] proliferation of small, technically-driven pilots across Asia and Africa – often testing similar applications" (Chamberlain, 2012[2]). Those leading innovation efforts within DAC members increasingly see it as important to "graduate" from implementing many micro-projects towards more meso- and large-scale programmes. However, this is not always straightforward. The middle ground between creative, high-risk but small-scale innovation projects, which can be seen as relatively unchallenging, and more conventional, low-risk, large-scale programmes, which are the norm for development and humanitarian donors, has not been effectively filled.

Initiatives such as challenge funds are a good example of such an emerging approach in practice. These funds increasingly recognise that significant gains are to be made in the middle "meso-zone" and require a forensic, focused and considered effort to bridge the gap through the application and take-up of evidence and research (see Box 4.2).

Box 4.2. DAC members' use of challenge funds as a means of strengthening implementation and evaluation

Challenge funds are one of the primary means by which Development Assistance Committee members engage in innovation activities, especially at cross-donor level. Prominent examples include the Global Innovation Fund (supported by the UK Department for International Development, the Swedish Ministry of Foreign Affairs/Sida (Swedish International Development Agency), the Australian Department of Foreign Affairs and Trade, and USAID among others). In 2018, Sida commissioned an evaluation of its investments in ten challenge funds over a decade. The results are relevant beyond Sida and for the donor community as a whole. Key lessons include:

- The rationale behind challenge funds includes using open competition to trigger innovative and cost-effective solutions to development challenges we do not have the answers for and mobilising private capital to match grants – innovation is a central component of these funds, which may choose to invest in existing, imported or tweaked solutions that need strengthening.

- The test for successful innovation should require that the solution be demonstrably more cost-effective than current mainstream practice in a given area, rather than simply the "newness" of the idea – the focus on effectiveness means that challenge funds can be a relevant mechanism for marshalling multiple organisations working on a single issue or problem towards a measurable outcome.

- For funds focused on innovation, it is important to be clear about the stage of innovation to be supported, what can realistically be achieved within the lifetime of the programme, what kind of technical assistance will be required to support innovators during programme implementation and what kind of additional support mechanisms may be required to support further development towards impact at scale – this may also include consideration of whether the challenge fund mechanism can deliver the desired development impact as a stand-alone programme or if it should be considered as a component of a more broadly focused programme.

- Challenge funds use a range of design features and direct interventions to ensure that funded projects have impact and are sustainable beyond the lifespan of the fund itself. All such interventions carry costs and involve trade-offs, as they require the fund managers to spend time and resources (either directly or by outsourcing to experts) on specific activities.

- Challenge funds are good at gathering evidence on "what works" around innovative solutions to development challenges, but not as good at using that knowledge productively. There is a notable imbalance between the effort devoted to seeding and testing new products, processes and services, and the limited focus on dissemination and uptake of these innovations.

- Despite greater focus among challenge funds towards actively fostering sustainability, with very limited exceptions, they do not use longitudinal studies conducted some three to five years after the end of project funding to track the outcomes and impact of fund activities; the absence of

---

> long-term tracking studies makes it difficult to conduct a definitive cost-benefit analysis of the effectiveness of different activities to support sustainability.
>
> - There are structural reasons why donors and fund managers focus on challenge fund design and implementation rather than long-term tracking and diffusion of ideas; in particular, donor funding tends to be short term and limited to the duration of particular programmes.
>
> Source: IPE Triple Line (2018[3]), *Evaluation of Sida's Global Challenge Funds: Lessons from a Decade Long Journey*, www.sida.se/contentassets/eb4c7e1c459a4ccbb8c3e6dbd1843219/2018_1_evaluation_of_sidas_global_challenge_funds.pdf.

All participating DAC member organisations flagged the evidence requirements of innovation efforts. There is not yet a culture of evidence-based innovation – evaluation and evidence are often absent. Different stages of the innovation process need distinct research approaches: early stages are typically about proof of concept; later stages require objective assessments of coverage and impact. In general, more work has been done on ex ante assessments to launch new pilots and rather less on ex post efforts to assess costs and benefits and make the argument for further testing and dissemination.

An interesting collaborative initiative underway at the time of writing is the DAC marker on innovation for development, which is currently being piloted across the DAC membership. This involves the design and testing of a systematic method of tracking innovation as proposed by Canada to the DAC Working Party on Development Finance Statistics in June 2018. The pilot, which ran over the course of 2019, tested the use of an innovation marker in the OECD Creditor Reporting System to allow DAC members and international stakeholders to identify and track innovation components of new projects in a systematic way.

The pilot's objective was two-fold:

1. to test the feasibility of identifying and tracking projects with an innovation component
2. to qualify the innovation component of the projects according to the proposed marker methodology.

Australia, Belgium, France and Slovenia are also piloting the innovation marker's feasibility and methodology in their international assistance programmes. Germany, Ireland, Sweden, the United Kingdom and the United States are closely following its evolution and engaging on an advisory basis. The overarching intent is to collect and generate data and learning, and disseminate knowledge, including from promising innovations that have the potential to scale for greater impact on poverty reduction.

Key issues for consideration

As noted above, there are challenges for donors in moving beyond micro-level pilot projects and initiatives that bundle together such projects. Pilotitis is not benign: it has led to waste, inefficiency and confusion across the sector, and in an infamous case involving mobile health innovations in Uganda, a government moratorium banned all new mobile phone-based innovation initiatives. However, moving into meso- and large-scale investments in innovation are not always straightforward, for a number of reasons:

- Transaction and staff costs at the meso- and large scales are relatively high: such initiatives can be low in terms of monetary investments required, but high in terms of staff time, and therefore do not align well with current donor imperatives around spend and "burn rates".
- Skills and capabilities are different to initial testing: as well as technical skills, there is a need for greater political and advocacy skills – these are not always easy to simply bring into an innovation project that is already underway.
- Resourcing: many existing funds compete to support early-stage innovations, leading to a recognised "valley of death" in financing beyond these stages.

- Evidence gaps: many pilots do not place enough emphasis on rigorous learning, so are not in a position to argue for greater resourcing.
- Institutional barriers: the point at which a promising innovation seems to have further scope is also where creative minorities have to face down vested interests that have more to gain from the status quo than from novel approaches.

Even in those DAC members where an evidence culture is relatively strong, the role of monitoring, evaluation and learning in innovation is weak at both project and portfolio levels. In general, innovation efforts are supported by favourable narratives and selective use of statistics rather than systematic analysis. Some innovation programmes use ideas from theories of change and theories of action to set out assumptions, hypotheses, comparative metrics of success and failure, and ideas for scaling strategies. But these tend to be the exceptions, not the rule.

How are innovations diffused, adopted and scaled?

This part of the innovation process sees solutions moving to widespread use through a variety of mechanisms, including open-source dissemination, replication, incorporation into government structures and commercialisation. Effective capabilities in diffusion, adoption and scale include dedicated resources and processes for demonstrating value added and making the case for diffusion and adoption; relevant investment in competencies and infrastructure to support scaling processes; and creating the space and scope for "creative destruction" of existing and established practices, and bringing about systemic changes in the organisation and its wider ecosystem.

Current state of play

The most widespread framework for the diffusion of innovations, developed by the scholar Everett Rogers, was informed by extensive studies and research in developing countries in the 1950s and 1960s, including Rogers' own work on agricultural extension services in rural areas. In part, at least, this was because "technology was assumed to be the heart of development" (Rogers, 2005[4]). But exactly how diffusion at scale is achieved is still something of an enigma in many development and humanitarian settings.

Where innovations have moved to scale in the sector, including across the case study countries, it can be attributed to a process of iterative, adaptive learning across three interlinked domains: 1) technical solutions; 2) organisational and business models; and 3) institutions, norms and politics. All of the most successful development and humanitarian innovations identified in the DAC peer learning exercise involved concerted efforts across all three of these domains.

Also, the work of Geoff Mulgan, former CEO of Nesta UK, sets out five distinct pathways to scale, as shown in Table 4.1. Lessons from across DAC members indicate that scaling up a development or humanitarian innovation to achieve impact often entails a combination of the strategies listed below, employed thoughtfully and persistently across the three domains over a sustained time period to build momentum, support and widespread adoption.

Table 4.1. Pathways of growth and replication

Pathways of growth and replication	
Advocacy	Spread through advocacy, persuasion and the sense of a movement; e.g. environmental non-profit response to acid rain pollution in the United States.
Networks	Grow through professional and other networks, helped by some evaluation; e.g. the 12-step programme of Alcoholics Anonymous.
Programmes	Replicate through programmes and partnerships, sometimes with payment, intellectual property, technical assistance and consultancy; e.g. Grameen Bank's replication within Bangladesh and then worldwide.
Direct control	Organic growth of a single organisation, sometimes including takeovers, sometimes with federated governance structure; e.g. Amnesty International or Greenpeace.

Source: Mulgan, G. et al. (2007[5]), Social Innovation: What It Is, Why It Matters and How It Can Be Accelerated, https://youngfoundation.org/wp-content/uploads/2012/10/Social-Innovation-what-it-is-why-it-matters-how-it-can-be-accelerated-March-2007.pdf.

Three of the case study countries – Australia, Sweden and the United Kingdom – have worked actively as members of the International Development Innovation Alliance (IDIA) network to establish a Working Group on Scaling Innovation. This group has established a set of common insights for funders seeking to take promising development innovations to scale.

These insights are organised into three discrete, yet complementary and interdependent, areas:

- First, dividing the scaling process into six overlapping stages, on a continuum from ideation through to sustainable scale.
- Second, eight good practices have been identified across these stages to help funders of development innovation enhance the impact of their support (Figure 4.1).
- Finally, a matrix of influencing factors that will either accelerate or constrain the scaling process has been created, with guidance on how funders can use these to initially assess – and continue to monitor – the scalability of an innovation over time.

Figure 4.1. IDIA good practices for funders in supporting scale

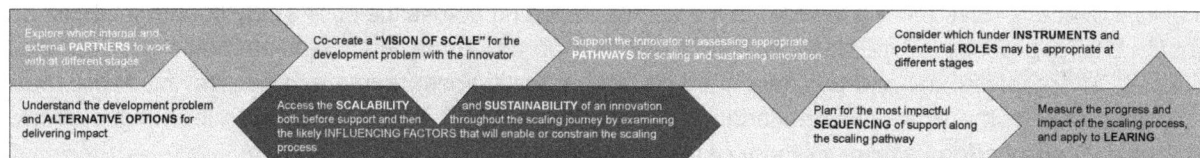

Source: IDIA (2017[6]), Insights on Scaling Innovation, https://static1.squarespace.com/static/5b156e3bf2e6b10bb0788609/t/5b1717eb8a922da5042cd0bc/1528240110897/Insights+on+Scaling+Innovation.pdf.

A key lesson for scaling work is that the wide-scale adoption of an innovation at the desired level of scale or exponential growth is shaped and influenced by the wider ecosystem of actors. The case studies show examples of donors actively considering and investing in innovation ecosystems at different levels. For example:

- global: Swedish and UK government investments in the Global Alliance for Humanitarian Innovation (now closed); national innovation hubs such as the United Kingdom's Global Disability and Innovation Hub; and those in the Netherlands, Norway, etc.
- national: innovation ecosystems in countries of the global South
- regional/local: innovation ecosystems in particular cities or regions.

These tend to be areas where there is a distinctive product (e.g. cholera vaccines, female contraceptives, vitamin-fortified seeds). However, ecosystems are also essential in areas where products have not yet emerged (e.g. treatments for Ebola) or in specific technological areas, most notably digital.

A number of the DAC members are also members of the "Million Lives Club", an initiative that highlights, catalogues and learns from the cohort of innovators whose efforts have reached a million or more end users. This is intended to serve as a kind of "S&P 500" for social impact, helping to promote successful scaling efforts and better connect innovators to potential scaling partners, such as local governments or impact investors.

Key issues for consideration

Across DAC members as a whole, greater effort is needed to reflect on the end-to-end process of innovation efforts and related outcomes. This means joining the dots between early-stage pilots and late-stage scaling; and thinking and learning more actively about innovation pathways as they are unfolding, and the factors and actors that enable or inhibit them.

While DAC members are tacitly aware of multiple pathways to scale, the rhetoric has focused on private sector replication. The reality is that there are many theories of scale, of which this is just one. It is vital that scaling efforts do not focus on just one as the dominant approach, as this would be counterproductive for individual innovation efforts and would undervalue the considerable innovation capabilities within the public and non-profit sectors.

At present, DAC members are not sufficiently joined up internally or externally when it comes to innovation efforts. Not enough attention is paid to how internal mechanisms can work to ensure testing and scaling of effective innovations; and, in particular, to establishing a clear link between funding innovations at one end of the pathway and being open to using purchasing power for proven innovations at the other.

While DAC members often celebrate effective innovations, these successes do not always lead to more systematic learning about innovation pathways. Often, staff members' grasp of how a particular innovation has moved from idea to scale is very simplistic and does not help others to grasp the particularities of the context, or to recognise the enablers of effective and practical application of novel and creative approaches. Building evidence on pathways to scale would benefit from a balanced examination of the successes that have already been achieved.

DAC members often fund all of the elements of an innovation ecosystem – research, education, skills, scholarships, programmes, partnerships, networks – but do not actively seek to optimise their different investments in a unified innovation approach. Such investment in ecosystems for transformative and anticipatory innovation is something that could be usefully undertaken across donors, to pool funds and reduce risks.

References

Chamberlain, S. (2012), *Pilot-itis: What's the Cure?*, BBC, http://www.bbc.co.uk/blogs/bbcmediaaction/entries/e00fc35a-0c0f-3e35-8280-38d048c34487 (accessed on 1 January 2020).   [2]

Global Emergency Group et al. (2017), *Global Prioritisation Exercise for Research and Innovation in the Humanitarian System: Phase One Mapping*, Elrha, Cardiff, http://www.elrha.org/researchdatabase/global-prioritisation-exercise-research-innovation-humanitarian-system-phase-one-mapping/ (accessed on 1 January 2020).   [1]

IDIA (2017), *Insights on Scaling Innovation*, International Development Innovation Alliance, https://static1.squarespace.com/static/5b156e3bf2e6b10bb0788609/t/5b1717eb8a922da5042cd0bc/1528240110897/Insights+on+Scaling+Innovation.pdf (accessed on 1 January 2020).   [6]

IPE Triple Line (2018), *Evaluation of Sida's Global Challenge Funds: Lessons from a Decade Long Journey*, Swedish International Development Agency, Stockholm, https://www.sida.se/contentassets/eb4c7e1c459a4ccbb8c3e6dbd1843219/2018_1_evaluation_of_sidas_global_challenge_funds.pdf (accessed on 1 January 2020).   [3]

Mulgan, G. et al. (2007), *Social Innovation: What It Is, Why It Matters and How It Can Be Accelerated*, The Young Foundation, https://youngfoundation.org/wp-content/uploads/2012/10/Social-Innovation-what-it-is-why-it-matters-how-it-can-be-accelerated-March-2007.pdf (accessed on 1 January 2020).   [5]

Rogers, E. (2005), *Diffusion of Innovations*, Free Press.   [4]

5 Next steps for Development Assistance Committee members

Although the development community has an established track record for innovating partnerships, funding instruments and technologies, they are not enough to deliver the Sustainable Development Goals. This chapter, organised around building blocks for innovation capabilities, provides recommendations on how innovation can best benefit poor and vulnerable people around the world for DAC members individually as well as collectively.

As set out in the introduction, innovation is of growing importance in development and humanitarian work. Numerous innovations have already had transformative effects on the lives of poor and vulnerable people around the world. The peer learning exercise (PLE) has identified promising efforts underway across the case study countries and among the OECD Development Assistance Committee (DAC) membership as a whole.

At its best, the innovation work DAC donors have led and supported involves the fusion of new technologies and technical advances with new business models and organisational approaches, and efforts to reform and transform institutions, norms and political contexts. It is through precisely such systemic efforts that we have seen the emergence and scaling of successful innovations such as new disease treatments, mobile financial services, and approaches to nutrition and resilience. Done poorly – which typically means an overt focus on technology, with insufficient attention to organisational and institutional contexts – innovation is not just ineffective, but can be harmful.

It is clear from the PLE that innovation for development is of growing importance to DAC members, individually and collectively. But to realise the broader ambitions of the innovation agenda, the DAC membership needs to build on the good work already underway to actively and sustainably encourage, incentivise and manage innovation efforts. This means supporting innovation not as a hoped-for result or another new sector of work, but as a centrally important and cross-cutting strategic capability; and harnessing this capability courageously and systematically in pursuit of the most pressing and complex development and humanitarian goals.

In this context, DAC members' collective innovation has a number of strengths:

- many transformative development and humanitarian efforts have already drawn on innovation approaches and thinking – from cash to microfinance to new vaccines
- among the most advanced members, the innovation approach is becoming more structured, systematic and goal-driven, especially at programme and project levels
- pockets of staff and teams across all of the case study countries, and more widely, feel empowered to take on board novel approaches, practices and ideas, and the language and concepts of innovation are becoming more widespread
- many joint efforts are underway across DAC members to strengthen innovation for development as a global public good, and the International Development Innovation Alliance (IDIA) network brings together many of the major players across the aid landscape for networking and shared learning.

There are also many opportunities for improvement:

- Greater clarity is needed on the goals and ambitions of innovation for development at institutional and sector-wide levels: what is innovation for, how will it work and why is it important?
- Gaps – in strategy, governance, management, co-ordination and process – should be addressed to strengthen internal coherence, institutional longevity, collective learning, and the external impact and sustainability of the innovation agenda.
- Organisational arrangements need strengthening: to improve signals, requirements and agreements between different internal teams and units pushing for similar institutional transformations.
- There is a need for more active efforts in evidence and learning, risk management, portfolio learning and management, and scaling, some of which are already underway.
- The lack of genuine and sustained engagement with the global South is a widespread problem, and should be addressed directly and collectively to ensure that innovation efforts are more relevant, appropriate and build on the best ideas from around the world.

The recommendations set out below provide a means for the DAC membership to build on their strengths and capitalise on these opportunities. Structured using the innovation capabilities framework (Figure 1.2) and the stages of strategic development (Table 2.1), these recommendations are presented with the aim of strengthening the innovation for development agenda, individually as well collectively, across DAC members in the form of a future agenda for an innovation workstream.

Table 5.1. Where are you in your innovation journey?

A: I am an emerging experimenter – You are a DAC member whose innovation work is relatively recent and small scale, linked to a specific programme or initiative such as health or job creation. Innovation is not yet the responsibility of a dedicated staff member, but might be part of a specific role.

B: I am a fast developer – You are a DAC member who has invested in a number of innovation programmes and made initial investments in innovation capacity. You have key individuals working to advise and support learning and networking, but are at a relatively early stage of institutional implementation and roll-out.

C: I am an established integrator – You are a DAC member who has a dedicated, recognised team and capability for innovation, and some form of strategic or policy framework, as well as a portfolio of investments in different areas.

D: I am a collaborative learner – You fit into one of the groups above and are especially keen to exploit the potential benefits of a collaborative and open approach to innovation across the DAC membership, and with the OECD Secretariat, building on the peer leaning experience.

A: I work for an emerging experimenter. What should I be considering?

Strategy, management and culture

1. Map out existing innovation work across the overall current portfolio of the organisation, including any thematic or geographic focus areas, and assess capabilities using the OECD self-assessment tool.

2. Assess both needs for innovation across partners and end users (external) and areas of technical potential (internal), and use the findings to develop a set of initial innovation priorities.

3. Explore the potential to deliver on these priorities by supporting both stand-alone and integrated innovation activities across the existing portfolio, as well as possible cross-DAC partnerships.

Organisation and collaboration for innovation

4. Identify a network of interested senior leaders and staff, and set up an innovation strategy event to facilitate dialogue on findings from the steps above; identify next steps and develop a roadmap for future work that includes roles and responsibilities.

5. Identify partners and mentors in learning from across the DAC and IDIA who can contribute to or partner on the prioritised next steps.

The innovation process

6. Work to pilot end-to-end evidence-based innovation management processes in high-priority areas of work.

7. Ensure innovation processes are inclusive of end users and Southern actors by default.

B and C: I work for a fast developer or an established integrator. What should I be considering?

Strategy, management and culture

1. Define a shared vision and strategy for innovation more clearly, setting out the what, who and how of innovation, with particular attention to the role of Southern actors and end users.

2. Set out clear incentives and drivers for innovation: be clear about the signals and requirements for innovation, and suggested entry points for staff and teams at different levels, functions and locations.

3. Work towards greater integration across innovation-related efforts, with greater and more lesson learning across sectors.

4. Make innovation the focus of an explicit organisational change campaign: look at all key processes in terms of how they enable or inhibit innovation and make adjustments, and join up efforts across dedicated innovation staff and other internal agents of change.

5. Build and support networks of internal innovation champions – at senior management and country levels, within technical or country groups, and among support and operational staff.

Organisation and collaboration for innovation

6. Make conscious use of innovation portfolio approaches to identify lessons, share experiences and track progress.

7. Improve governance of innovation at senior management level, to ensure a high-level overview of and deliberation on the overall innovation portfolio – clearly signal the level of ambition and appetite for risk to the organisation.

8. Develop more coherent and courageous narratives about innovation risk and acceptability, and the different kinds of risk that can be alternately embraced, tolerated and minimised in innovation processes.

9. Consider the role of existing partners in developing and rolling out new ideas and approaches.

10. Actively seek to engage actors in and from the global South throughout the lifecycle of innovation processes and programmes.

The innovation process

11. Invest in innovation skills for new and existing staff members at different levels: focus on innovation management for general staff, and innovation technical advisory capacities of dedicated innovation staff.

12. Ensure stronger and more systematic reflection, evidence, documentation, data and communication of lessons across innovation processes, within specific programmes and across innovation portfolios as a whole, and make inclusion of end users and Southern actors a key criterion for assessments.

13. Build stronger processes and mechanisms for integrating outcomes of successful innovation efforts with mainstream programming efforts.

14. Invest in co-creation efforts in relation to complex intractable challenges; in particular, place greater emphasis on country-level programming efforts in innovation as a means of bringing in promising innovations and innovators from the global South.

D: I want to engage more across the DAC membership and with the OECD Secretariat. What should I be considering?

The suggestions below are made based on the assumption that DAC members and the OECD Secretariat will be working in close collaboration with and as part of existing cross-organisational networks on innovation, including the IDIA.

Strategy, management and culture

1. Work to establish a champions group of senior leaders on innovation for development, bringing together heads of DAC members to advocate for more and better innovation processes and outcomes.

2. Provide a standing hub or platform to join up, co-ordinate and shape innovation activities at the strategic level across the development sector as a whole, paying particular attention to the innovation gap the Sustainable Development Goals (SDGs) and humanitarian resources face, anticipatory and transformative innovation, ongoing work on research for innovation, and cross-organisational capacity-strengthening efforts.

3. Develop a shared global narrative or statement on innovation in development and humanitarian work: what it is, why it matters, and how best to enable and support it.

Organisation and collaboration for innovation

4. Explore the potential for collective approaches to tracking and learning from innovation efforts, building on the ongoing DAC innovation marker work and emerging efforts in portfolio-wide learning.

5. Work to bring actors from the global South – from national governments to the private sector, civil society and poor communities – into a more central role in the innovation for development ecosystem; actively bridge gaps between innovation efforts in the global North and South.

6. Work in close collaboration and partnership with key innovation players externally and internally, including the IDIA; Global Innovation Exchange; the OECD Observatory of Public Sector Innovation (OPSI); and the OECD Directorate for Science, Technology and Innovation, to ensure the benefits of collective action are realised and duplication avoided.

The innovation process

7. Facilitate efforts across DAC members to establish and accelerate shared work on development challenges that demand radically new, anticipatory and transformative innovation.

8. Invest in enhanced monitoring, evaluation and learning for innovation efforts in collaboration with the DAC Network on Development Evaluation and the Results Community and within the DAC Peer Review process.

Annex A. Draft OECD-DAC self-assessment tool on innovation capabilities

Innovation for development has many dimensions that Development Assistance Committee members need to understand and explore.

Figure A.1. Innovation capabilities framework: The building blocks of innovation for development and humanitarian work

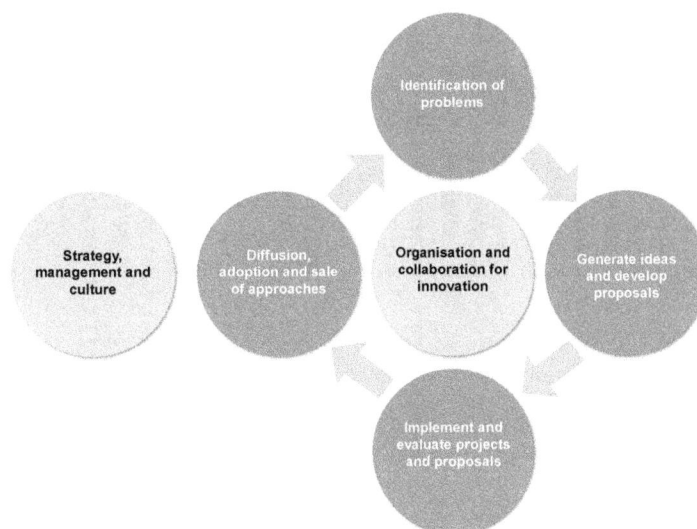

For each of these capabilities, three broad stages of development are articulated to enable reflection and self-assessment:

- Initial application: a general understanding of what the specific innovation capability is about and how it applies in a development and humanitarian context.
- Emerging capability: skills applied in an occasional fashion or in a "low-intensity" manner, that allows staff to experiment with using them in a safe and/or controlled fashion.
- Established practice: skill applied in a deep systematic way across a range of areas and is part of "how things are done".

Table A.1. Self-assessment tool on innovation capabilities

Innovation capability	Specific organisational practices	Key questions	Level of progress	Narrative description
Strategy, management and culture	Strategy, leadership and management	Is there an innovation strategy? How is it linked to the overall corporate strategy? How well are innovation goals articulated in relation to development ambitions? Do innovation goals allow space for creativity and contextualised approaches? What is the role of senior leaders and managers in driving and encouraging innovation across the department? Who takes responsibility for innovation across the department? Is there explicit attention to how existing modalities, procedures and processes might inhibit innovation, and efforts underway to address or mitigate these issues?	Initial application	There are ongoing discussions about developing an innovation for development strategy. Innovation is viewed as the responsibility of a specific role or roles, either within dedicated teams or specific technical areas (e.g. health). Some managers give people the time to innovate, but there is not always consistent support from the top. Some leaders talk the talk, but do not always walk the walk. Organisational processes sometimes enable, sometimes inhibit, innovation efforts.
			Emerging capability	An innovation strategy exists but is not well integrated with overall development or departmental goals. Attention is being paid to innovation at the front line of development and humanitarian work and how to best foster and facilitate it. Leaders and managers increasingly ask for and exhibit innovation approaches and acknowledge staff and partners for using such approaches. There is growing attention to the need to adapt organisational processes and procedures to better enable innovation, and reforms are underway.
			Established practice	Innovation is established within the overall corporate strategy and viewed as essential for achieving long- and short-term development and humanitarian goals. Leaders and managers recognise and reinforce the link between innovation and development effectiveness. Managers regularly apply relevant tools and techniques, and act as innovation role models. Leaders demonstrate they are more interested in learning from failure than in punishing it. Organisational processes have taken into account the needs of the innovation agenda, and key barriers have been addressed in a systematic fashion.
	Culture, capacity and mindset	How does the department deal with risk taking in the context of innovation? Is there a culture of rewarding and supporting innovation? How well do human resources practices support and enable a culture of innovation? What efforts are made to build staff capacity in innovation?	Initial application	There is emerging recognition of the need for new ways of tackling development and humanitarian goals. The approach to risk taking is ad hoc and varies from team to team and office to office. Key job descriptions and appraisals make reference to innovation and creativity as an important capability. Partners are assessed on the basis of their innovative capabilities. Staff learning on innovation is informal and primarily driven by individual motivation.
			Emerging capability	There is a widely accepted view that the department needs to explore new ways of tackling development challenges. There is an emerging framework for understanding and managing risk associated with novelty – new ideas are not rejected prematurely. There are rewards and incentives for innovation for staff and partners alike. There is investment for innovation capacities for select staff dedicated to innovation.
			Established practice	The department is seen as fostering and supporting innovative ideas and approaches from diverse sources, inside and outside. Staff and partners across policy, technical and operational roles feel able to try out new ideas. There is a systematic approach to assessing and managing risk. Innovation capacities are considered a core staff capacity, with commensurate investment in formal and informal learning approaches.

Category	Dimension	Questions	Level	Description
Identification of problems	Observing and listening	How are innovation-related problems, needs and opportunities identified? Who is involved and in what ways?	Initial application	Efforts are underway within the innovation for development initiative to consult with internal colleagues and existing stakeholders and partners about potential opportunities for improvement as well as seeking out ideas for where innovation is most needed.
		How are end users and national/local actors involved in determining needs and opportunities? What is the role of research, learning and consultation processes in determining innovation needs, opportunities and priorities?	Emerging capability	The innovation for development programme proactively seeks out feedback about opportunities and challenges from a wide range of stakeholders, with a growing focus on end users and other actors in developing countries, and systematically analyses that feedback for ideas. Research plays an important role in learning about problems and challenges. There are technology-specific learning efforts underway, although it is accepted that technology alone is insufficient to enable change.
		How does the department expand its understanding and capabilities in different technologies (e.g. digital, frontier technologies, etc.)?	Established practice	The innovation effort has well-established evidence-based and creative processes to discover and explore new ideas and approaches. Novel methods and technologies such as immersions, crowdsourcing and text mining are used to gain insight. Strong emphasis is placed on using research to understand the experiences of end users, to unpack long-standing development challenges to explore the potential of new ideas, processes and technologies, and as a way of catalysing novel thinking.
	Questioning and challenging	How well does the department support questioning of and suggested alternatives to standard operating procedures, within and outside the organisational boundaries? (demand for novelty) How are staff, partners and wider stakeholders encouraged to learn and go beyond existing ideas and approaches? (supply of novelty)	Initial application	There is growing understanding that there are potentially viable alternatives to current ways of working and effort to understand the relative strengths and weaknesses of each.
			Emerging capability	The department encourages staff to assess the limitations of their own knowledge and practice and find opportunities to learn more. There is recognition of the value of "unlearning" previously acquired knowledge, practices and ways of thinking that are no longer applicable or relevant in different contexts or for new and emerging challenges and problems.
		In what ways can and have the status quo of existing practices been changed as a result of the innovation for development effort?	Established practice	The department and relevant partners, both through the innovation for development effort and more broadly, routinely reflect on what lessons have been learnt from ongoing efforts, and use this reflection to question assumptions and current practices. Staff in the department and key innovation partners are supported to be open to new ideas and thinking no matter where they come from, and to actively consider the possibilities and opportunities new ideas present for programmes, policies and procedures. Questioning the status quo in productive and constructive ways is increasingly encouraged and supported.
Generation of ideas and development of proposals	Exploring and scanning for ideas and solutions	How does the department seek out new ideas and solutions to development challenges?	Initial application	The innovation for development effort, the department as a whole and relevant partners are starting to understand that other organisations and sectors can have different, but relevant, approaches for tackling development and humanitarian challenges.
		How does the department identify innovators and innovations inside and outside the department?	Emerging capability	There is ongoing effort to engage with individuals and teams internally and externally who are undertaking innovative work and investing time in finding out what they do and how they do it, identifying what is different about their approach and what can be learnt for more general application.
		What resources are used for exploring and scanning for solutions? How does the department engage with national and local actors in identifying new ideas and proposals?	Established practice	The department and partners use networks, research and other resources to identify and prioritise both the most important challenges as well as to scan for potential solutions and approaches. There is active investment in bringing in individuals and teams from different organisations, sectors, locations/countries who can be a source of innovative ideas, who can identify alternative options based on their practice, and who can support innovation efforts.

		Maturity	Description
Crafting new proposed approaches	How does the department and its partners make use of prototyping, design thinking, human-centred design, user-driven design, etc. to develop and test new ideas in development and humanitarian contexts? Who is involved in processes to develop new approaches, and in what ways? How do development processes engage with end users and stakeholders in developing countries?	Initial application	Staff and partners within the innovation for development effort and more widely understand how crafting processes and approaches can be used to bring new ideas to life and to explore how new ideas might work in practice.
		Emerging capability	The department increasingly uses design and innovation management processes that help internal and external stakeholders visualise a product or service, to identify potential opportunities and challenges. These are used to explain or test out approaches with colleagues, partners and users. Prototyping is actively undertaken in development and humanitarian contexts.
		Established practice	Prototyping is undertaken routinely with a wide constellation of stakeholders, including internal staff, end users and developing country partners, as a means of developing new products, services and business processes and to gather feedback on feasibility, relevance and potential value. Staff and partners understand how to refine and improve prototypes to address emerging issues and to improve the potential for impact and scale.
Implementation and evaluation of projects and processes — Piloting and experimenting	How are new ideas applied and tested in the context of innovation programmes? What innovation management methods and tools are used? How is innovation managed as an end-to-end process?	Initial application	The department understands the process of managing innovations in development and humanitarian work. There are different kinds of stage-gate approaches being used in innovation efforts. There is understanding of the importance of starting small and systematically learning to demonstrate potential value.
		Emerging capability	There is understanding of the different skills, processes, partners and resources needed for distinct stages of the innovation piloting and experimentation process. There is acceptance that pilots need to be designed with a focus on both visibility and winning hearts and minds. Failure is not automatically seen as the death of an idea, but as a catalyst for sustained efforts.
		Established practice	Piloting processes are focused on assessing the broader viability and longer term sustainability of new ideas. The department supports the use of flexible financing and adaptive programming approaches to navigate valleys of death. Piloting is seen as an essential component of the wider culture of experimentation.
Test, evaluate and learn	How does evaluation, research and learning feature in the innovation process? What kinds of research and learning tools and methods are used across the innovation cycle to demonstrate the evidence base for new innovative solutions? In what ways is evidence used to make the case for sustained investment and to justify scaling of successful innovations?	Initial application	There is growing understanding about how tests and experiments can examine what works and what does not. There is awareness that this has resource implications, and initial efforts are being made to invest in monitoring, evaluation and learning alongside innovation investments.
		Emerging capability	The department ensures innovation programmes and projects include sufficient time, resources and an appropriate mix of methodologies for testing and evaluation, across different stages of a project's or service's lifecycle. It is widely accepted that pilots work best when coupled with a continuous assessment of impacts and the ability to adjust and correct on the fly.
		Established practice	The department actively promotes the use of large-scale assessments and evaluative thinking as a core innovation capability. There is evidence of use of a mix of methods (including A/B testing, randomised control trials, user feedback and systems thinking) to gain evidence about what works, why and in what circumstances. Innovation is underpinned by an approach of continuous improvement.

Category	Questions	Maturity level	Description
Diffusion, adoption and scale of approaches / Communication and advocacy	How are the results of new innovations communicated and championed in the department?	Initial application	Efforts are made to communicate innovation results beyond pilot teams and early adopters. There is proactive exploration of the possibility of applying specific innovations in new relevant contexts. However, whether a particular innovation is accepted comes largely down to personal networks and chance.
	Are there well-established processes and approaches for communicating innovation successes and failures? How do technical and operational cadres and teams engage with the results of innovation efforts?	Emerging capability	Work is underway to develop coalitions of the willing testers to share experiences and catalyse further applications and results. Efforts are communicated to potential supporters and champions, who become actively engaged in making the case for greater investment and change. Quick wins are identified thanks to evidence and learning processes.
	What is the role of senior leaders and champions in ensuring institutional attention and related learning?	Established practice	The department is committed to using the outputs of innovation processes. There are accepted mechanisms and processes for assessing the viability of particular innovations. Well-specified processes exist for submitting and assessing particular innovations and approving their wider use. There are established events and processes for promoting awareness of specific innovations and innovation in general.
Adoption, application and systems change	How does the department support and invest in innovation scaling?	Initial application	The department is experimenting with a range of relevant approaches that can be used to take a particular innovation to scale. Innovators are asked to consider adoption and scale from the outset of an innovation process. This includes initial consideration of how approaches can be integrated into departmental programming.
	What models and tools are used by staff and partners to ensure scaling?	Emerging capability	The department is aware of the implications of adoption and scaling for existing practices and processes and actively explores ways of enabling adoption and scale from the outset of innovation processes. Programming efforts actively seek to use innovative approaches.
	How are the skills and capacities for scaling and adoption supported and strengthened?	Established practice	Specific scaling mechanisms and business models are established and accepted by the department, and necessary skills, capacities and relationships are in place to facilitate their application. There are established processes for making and communicating the business case for widespread adoption of specific tested innovations. Innovation is a key consideration throughout the programme cycle.
Organisation and collaboration for innovation / Innovation portfolio management and learning	How is the overall innovation portfolio considered and managed? How are different types and levels of innovation considered (e.g. incremental to radical, etc.)?	Initial application	There is recognition of the need to look across the overall innovation portfolio to determine progress and priorities. Some initial cross-portfolio work is happening. Active learning is happening across sectors, themes and goals.
		Emerging capability	There are regular cross-portfolio review and reflection sessions to review and learn from ongoing efforts, and share good practices and lessons across projects.
	How strategic and coherent is the portfolio, and how is the overall alignment managed? How does cross-portfolio learning work, and with what outcomes?	Established practice	There are strategic planning, design and refresh processes focused on the overall innovation portfolio strategy. Work is underway to define priorities, align outcomes and allocate resources for new funding cycles and opportunities. There is effort to rationalise, combine and integrate efforts across the innovation work of the department. Work is underway to align performance indicators and aggregate monitoring data across the portfolio through a shared management information and system.

Networking, collaboration and partnership		
How does collaboration for innovation work across the department? Which actors are involved in innovation programmes and in what ways? What is the specific role of end users and national/local actors? How are goals and objectives of innovation collaborations co-created, and with what benefits? What efforts are being made in open innovation across existing development and humanitarian stakeholders? How do implementing partner arrangements enable and incentivise innovation? How are innovation partnerships conceptualised, designed and implemented?	Initial application	There is recognition that collaboration internally and with others can improve the chances for success and provide a safe space to explore ideas and ask questions. There is initial engagement on innovation issues across different organisational silos as well as with other donors, traditional development players and new actors. For the most part, the networking used to achieve goals in based on individual trust rather than organisational arrangements.
	Emerging capability	Staff and partners are using multi-stakeholder networks and working groups to get results. Peers are helping peers across organisational boundaries. Formal collaboration mechanisms are being created and recognised, including partnership agreements. Open innovation is increasingly recognised as vital to the innovation effort, and the department works to foster this across its partners, grantees and with other donors. It is seen as important to develop a vision, narrative and message that all stakeholders involved in innovation efforts share and jointly own, and some efforts are working toward this.
	Established practice	Collaboration is a defining principle across the department. A range of internal and external collaboration mechanisms operate, with clearly defined roles and responsibilities in terms of the organisational goals. Some develop collaboration capability within the department while others have a clear focus. It is common to share people and resources to enable joint ownership and delivery of innovation initiatives, programmes or projects. There are well-established protocols for negotiating and establishing multi-stakeholder partnerships for innovation.

Annex B. Peer learning country case studies

Country case study: Australia

In 2019, the OECD facilitated a peer learning exercise on innovation in development and humanitarian work to support member states working to transform their efforts and impacts. The peer learning mission took place in Canberra, Australia in November 2019 and focused on the Australian Department of Foreign Affairs and Trade (DFAT) and staff and partners. The peer learning facilitators involved were from France, New Zealand and the OECD Observatory of Public Sector Innovation (OPSI) Secretariat.

Innovation strategy plays out at a number of different levels in DFAT. They include:

- at the level of the whole of government (Australia Innovates agenda)
- department wide (as articulated in the 2017 white paper Opportunity, Security, Strength)
- the InnovationXchange (iXc) innovation programme (DFAT innovation strategy 2018-21 and related learning agenda)
- by technology area (e.g. cybersecurity or technology for development)
- by intervention (e.g. a particular innovation effort consisting of a package of interventions)
- by specific experiment (e.g. a particular pilot testing out new approaches).

There is a good level of coherence in messaging and concepts across these levels. The iXc-led innovation strategy is especially strong in terms of theories and assumptions about how innovation will contribute to institutional change and the focus on capacities (which has inspired OECD work, including the current peer learning exercise).

There are signs of an emerging overarching language that brings different innovation narratives together, as described in the 2017 white paper:

- new and adapted technologies
- new and adapted financial and business models
- new partnerships, collaborations and relationships
- new and improved internal working practices and processes.

Lessons on culture, capacity and mindset

The drivers of innovation are seen as clear, in terms of transforming practices and impacts, and these were seen as creating the space for innovation. The risk appetite for novel and experimental approaches varies considerably between teams, units, functions, embassies and partners.

There is good work by iXc to build capacity in innovation. Both technically oriented staff (in areas such as health, humanitarian and governance) and more process-oriented staff (in policy, evaluation and results) shared a strong interest in strengthening skills in specific innovation processes and mechanisms (e.g. running a challenge, brokering innovation partnerships) and general skills (e.g. thinking more creatively about existing challenges, thinking about and navigating complex problems).

Across teams and units such as procurement, development effectiveness and learning, there was a real sense of energy and enthusiasm to support innovation and there is positive work underway to create space and opportunity through design and procurement trials.

Lessons on organisation for innovation

Over the course of its existence, iXc has been seen alternately as owner, champion and enabler of innovation. The shift from being a 'vertical' implementer of innovation programmes and projects to a more 'horizontal' enabler of others' innovation efforts is an important transition and the enabling role is a vital one for the future innovation trajectory.

Staff across DFAT appreciate the role of iXc as a change maker, facilitator and provider of capacity and expertise. The investment in iXc over time is paying dividends and should be capitalised upon by DFAT as a whole, both in the context of the new aid policy and in the overall work on foreign affairs and trade. An analogy with human resource functions is pertinent: while human resources are undertaken by all staff, you still need a central team to support, steward and guide activities. While innovation belongs to everyone, there is an important role for iXc to play in strengthening the organisation, capacity and culture around innovation.

Lessons on collaboration for innovation

There are good and open relationships between DFAT, iXc and the wider Australian and global development innovation ecosystems – whether through bringing in private sector expertise, university and academic skills; other donors; or other Australian government agencies and innovation networks. It was especially good to see the number of individual innovators who have received support from iXc and related resources.

Lessons on the innovation process

The innovation programme as a whole has a very thoughtful and systematic approach to its theory of change, thanks to the 2018-21 strategy. There is a very welcome emphasis on testing, evaluating and learning at the level of iXc's overall innovation strategy. Few donors have explored their innovation work so frequently and consistently as DFAT.

Across DFAT as a whole there is a lot of enthusiasm for generating creative solutions to external and internal problems. A lot of informal work is done by individuals inside and outside the organisation who have personal experience of a particular challenge and are keen to identify novel solutions.

As well as focusing on developing ideas for innovation, there are emerging opportunities for embedding innovation in wider programme proposal processes. DFAT's innovation work has been very good at establishing a range of small-scale creative pilots in particular countries to address a range of development challenges as well as within the department itself on internal organisational processes. A few have reached regional scale, especially in the digital space and health data apps. A number of larger-scale programmes are working in highly experimental ways in terms of who they work with, how they work and what they do.

Through the work of iXc and its influence on the rest of the organisation – as well as the Australian government's wider interest and focus on innovation – DFAT has improved its ability to tell innovation success stories inside and outside the organisation. Particularly noteworthy is the attention DFAT's work has gained by winning awards for innovation. It is clear that development innovations capture the imagination of the wider Australian public service.

At the tacit level, especially within the iXc and among key collaborators across DFAT, there is a clear sense of the diversity of pathways to scale – whether through getting an idea taken up across a particular programme or across DFAT, or by a partner government, by private sector commercialisation, by open source replication and so on. Many respondents and interviewees saw DFAT's role as helping 'make maps', and guiding innovators on the pathway to scale and in some cases re-shaping the enabling environment, or 'innovation ecosystem'.

Country case study: France

Background

In 2019, the OECD facilitated a peer learning exercise on innovation in development and humanitarian work to support member states working to transform their efforts and impacts. The peer learning mission took place in Paris, France in July 2019 and focused on both the French Ministry of Foreign Affairs and the French Development Agency (Agence Française de Développement, AFD) staff and partners. The peer learning facilitators involved were from Switzerland, the United Kingdom and the OECD Development Assistance Committee (DAC) Secretariat.

Lessons on strategy, leadership and management

In the Ministry of Europe and Foreign Affairs, the innovation agenda is driven by the sense that foreign affairs must become more open, creative and technologically savvy. These ideas were articulated by those working directly on innovation issues – whether the innovation team, or specific units such as the Office of the Ambassador for Cyber and Digital Issues.

Innovation is very much an emerging movement in the Ministry of Europe and Foreign Affairs, with a few bright spots and a number of significant successes in areas such as development, health, finance innovations and agricultural research. In AFD, innovation for development is the focus of concerted and rapid efforts. An emergent strategy has coalesced into an impressive start-up approach. Innovation was introduced formally into the AFD agenda in 2017. The department has made rapid and extensive progress, thanks to a coherent set of messages, clear senior management buy-in, and an energetic and dedicated team.

Lessons on culture, capacity and mindset

In the Ministry of Europe and Foreign Affairs, innovative approaches to diplomacy have traction and reinforce the overall innovation for development narrative. Innovation is a part of its overall advocacy and influencing work.

In AFD, innovation has captured leaders' imaginations and ideas, and is seen as speaking to the future of the organisation. There is evidence of enthusiastic, skilled, critical self-reflection around innovation. There is also a conscious effort to build the capacity of staff through formal training and mentoring, targeting both those who have received innovation funds through the intrapreneur scheme and those interested in innovation and design more generally.

Lessons on organisation for innovation

In the Ministry of Europe and Foreign Affairs, the development policy team focuses on different aspects of innovation, playing an advocacy role at the international level, an arms-length enabling role for the ecosystem and a more direct catalytic role for specific changes.

In AFD, the innovation unit plays an active role, engaging with internal departments and innovators based in headquarters and country offices. The innovation unit is also building a diverse portfolio in terms of thematic areas and the focus of each effort.

Lessons on collaboration for innovation

Extensive work is being done in the Ministry of Europe and Foreign Affairs to cultivate and connect innovators in the French ecosystem with actors in developing countries and to support specific ecosystems in developing countries. This means building relationships with decision makers; designing targeted events and workshops to spur new international partnerships; organising missions to familiarise innovators, researchers and companies with new opportunities; matching individuals, institutions and companies with international partners; and acting as an international portal for the French innovation system.

In AFD, collaborations are instrumental, and geared towards specific innovation processes and potential partners to take those new ideas forward.

Lessons on the innovation process

The Ministry of Europe and Foreign Affairs is working in different sectors to understand innovation systems, spot opportunities for and barriers to novel approaches, and communicate them to interested organisations.

The Ministry of Europe and Foreign Affairs is actively working to scale ideas from within the French innovation ecosystem that might have traction in developing country contexts, many of them digital in nature. Work is underway to develop, co-develop or identify external resources to help secure and scale promising collaborations and find ways to accelerate innovation processes. The ministry is also looking for ways to better support the commercialisation of research and build international partnerships that create global opportunities for innovative ideas.

AFD uses a range of approaches to identify problems and establish how best to work on them. Some of these are competitive internally and externally and there is a clear focus on identifying and working with the best ideas. There are also numerous examples of working with end users and new stakeholders – including poor communities, municipal authorities or private sector organisations in developing countries.

AFD has well-developed practices to design pilot programmes and to win support and engagement across the organisation. This involves articulating a clear, step-by-step process for innovation efforts to show how they can go from an initial idea to having an impact on the organisation.

Country case study: Sweden

Background

In 2019, the OECD facilitated a peer learning exercise on innovation in development and humanitarian work to support member states working to transform their efforts and impacts. The peer learning mission took place in Stockholm, Sweden in October 2019 and focused on both the Swedish Ministry of Foreign Affairs and the Swedish International Development Agency (Sida) staff and partners. The peer learning facilitators involved were from Canada, Iceland, the Netherlands and the OECD DAC Secretariat.

Lessons on strategy, leadership and management

Sweden is in the leading tier of innovation donors. Through Sida it is involved in many joint efforts to strengthen innovation for development as a global public good, such as the Global Innovation Fund, Grand Challenges initiatives and sector-wide innovation-driven efforts in energy and health. It has also played an important role as the first mover on a number of transformative development innovations, from cash to microfinance to new vaccines.

At senior level, there is a vision of what innovation can amount to, whether it is transforming efforts to achieve the United Nations Sustainable Development Goals or supporting national innovation ecosystems to enable truly locally led development. Across the Ministry for Foreign Affairs and Sida, there is a sense of positivity and optimism about innovation, which is shared by other governmental actors in the Swedish innovation ecosystem.

Lessons on culture, capacity and mindset

There is a long-held sense that Sida and the Ministry for Foreign Affairs culture is open and flexible, and can create a space for innovation, as well as being receptive to new modalities and capacities, such as agile and adaptive management, that support innovation.

Sida is perceived internally – as in the donor and wider development community – to be open to ideas and principles of being a 'learning organisation'.

Across Sida and the Ministry for Foreign Affairs, innovation underpins the things staff members are most proud of in their work. This extends beyond innovations that individuals have worked on directly – there was a clear collective sense of achievement from innovation efforts.

Lessons on organisation for innovation

Internally, a range of mechanisms and efforts support innovation, including the research portfolio, challenge funds and specific initiatives such as Power Africa.

There are numerous examples of individual development and humanitarian change agents working out of both the Ministry for Foreign Affairs and Sida who have followed their passion to make innovation count – from the technological (solar power for refugee camps) to the social (behavioural approaches to tackling women's economic empowerment).

There is also a genuinely supportive environment internally – in terms of flexibility, effectiveness and doing things better – and externally – in terms of the innovation landscape in Sweden and the broader political support for innovation in Sweden.

Innovation capacity strengthening is informal and tacit, relying on social networks, or down to individual educational histories.

Lessons on collaboration for innovation

Within challenge funds, the private sector is held by respondents to be the 'partner of choice'. Sida is also a natural partner for academics and researchers because of its reflective culture.

The Swedish donor system is highly collaborative when it comes to other donors. Many of the large-scale efforts have come from working with others: Global Innovation Fund, Power Africa and challenge funds.

Many parallel innovation programmes work with the same partners, so there is scope to bring partners together across the portfolio as a whole.

Lessons on the innovation process

At the outset of specific innovation initiatives, there have been efforts to engage with Swedish, international and national stakeholders – ranging from the private sector to civil society and other donors – to learn about their ideas.

When it comes to developing innovative solutions to development and humanitarian problems, in both the Ministry for Foreign Affairs and Sida there is a growing movement to hear and listen more to other stakeholders, especially in the wider Swedish innovation ecosystem.

The Sida Lab is a promising new development with the potential to take forward a number of these areas. Specifically, the Sida Lab is intended to be a support structure for innovative initiatives such as new modalities or forms of co-operation across Sida including embassies, who can apply for funds and technical advice. The specific focus is on initiatives with the potential to speed up the implementation of Agenda 2030, in particular those initiatives which emphasise experimentation, co-creation and continuous learning with partners.

Externally, Sida and the Ministry of Foreign Affairs take into account aspects of innovation ecosystems in their work; for example, investing research systems across Africa or on all the components of innovation in a country such as Rwanda, from development programming, research investments, private sector investments, PhD scholarship schemes and digital capability strengthening schemes.

Country case study: United Kingdom

Background

In 2019, the OECD facilitated a peer learning exercise on innovation in development and humanitarian work to support member states working to transform their efforts and impacts. The peer learning mission took place in London, England in July 2019 and focused on the Department for International Development (DFID) staff and partners. The peer learning facilitators involved were from Australia, Austria and France.

Lessons on strategy, leadership and management

There are many co-existing narratives on innovation, with a highly decentralised approach to undertaking innovation efforts, in keeping with other areas of DFID's work.

Greater clarity on how innovation issues feed into and are decided on at the senior levels of the organisation would be a valuable means of strengthening innovation governance.

At middle management level, and within specific teams and units, levels of support and enthusiasm for innovation for development are high.

Lessons on culture, capacity and mindset

Aspects of DFID's organisational culture support the innovation for development agenda. Staff with entrepreneurial mindsets and mentalities can pursue their intrinsic motivations for being in international development and humanitarian work, and for many this means finding creative and novel solutions to long-standing problems.

There is an open-minded, evidence-based culture where questioning is encouraged at all levels. This is further facilitated by DFID's work on adaptive management and the opportunity for staff to tap into support structures to design and implement programmes much more flexibly.

Among the converted, there is a strong shared belief in the potential of innovation to improve development and humanitarian practices and results. Internally, programmes with innovation components are widely shared and celebrated, and in turn build support for innovation.

Operational functions – such as compliance, legal and procurement functions – enable innovation because of informal relationships and trust between would-be innovators and relevant staff. There is scope to build on informal good practices with systematic adjustments to structures, processes and procedures.

Lessons on organisation

Innovation is a set of highly dispersed and diffuse approaches undertaken by the Research and Evidence Division, the Emerging Policy and Innovation Capability team in Policy Division, country offices and technical cadres.

Innovation is organised along similar lines to specific themes within development (such as climate or gender) which needs to be mainstreamed, as opposed to a core organisational capability or ambition (such as strategy, value for money or accountability). Internally, personal alliances play a central role in joining up work and making it coherent.

Lessons on collaboration for innovation

The private sector is a key partner of choice and there is also some engagement with existing partners such as civil society, the United Nations and international financial institutions.

There is growing awareness of the need for appropriate business models for developing, testing and scaling effective innovations and work is underway to develop public private partnerships for innovation.

DFID is exemplary when it comes to working with other donors in pursuit of innovation – for example, working on joint challenge funds, developing new principles in areas such as digital, engaging with new and emerging areas for innovation such as disability inclusion, or tackling modern slavery.

Lessons on the innovation process

DFID is good at generating ideas and designing programmes and projects. There are very good technical skills among programme, research and advisory staff and the organisation puts a strong emphasis on good evidence-based design processes. Many innovation programmes are funded through the Research and Evidence Division. There is much scope for the Research and Evidence Division's advisors to identify innovation opportunities in an entrepreneurial fashion, to seek out possible areas for action and to use evidence to make the case for backing innovation approaches. Innovation problems are also identified in a meaningful way in country-level 'exemplar programmes' in innovation.

The mentality and mindset for undertaking pilots and experimenting are well established in DFID. The organisation supports these activities in various ways, though adaptive management, organisational agility and innovation management.

There is scope for further improvement of innovation governance processes across DFID departments as well as clarity on roles and responsibilities to further advance DFID's internal innovation capability and its investments in different forms of innovation to advance development outcomes.

DFID has a good system for testing, evaluating and learning. Although it is not perfect, as a donor DFID's evidence culture is relatively strong. There is a need for innovation in monitoring, evaluation and learning to best support innovation, which requires supplementing ex-ante and ex-post monitoring, evaluation and learning with more operational research approaches that support real-time and ongoing decision making and learning.

While the organisation engages with other donors, United Kingdom civil society, the private sector, academia and innovation intermediaries in a meaningful way, the role of actors from the Global south risks being overlooked and neglected.